THE HOOTERS COOKBOOK

The Original Hooters®
in Clearwater, Florida

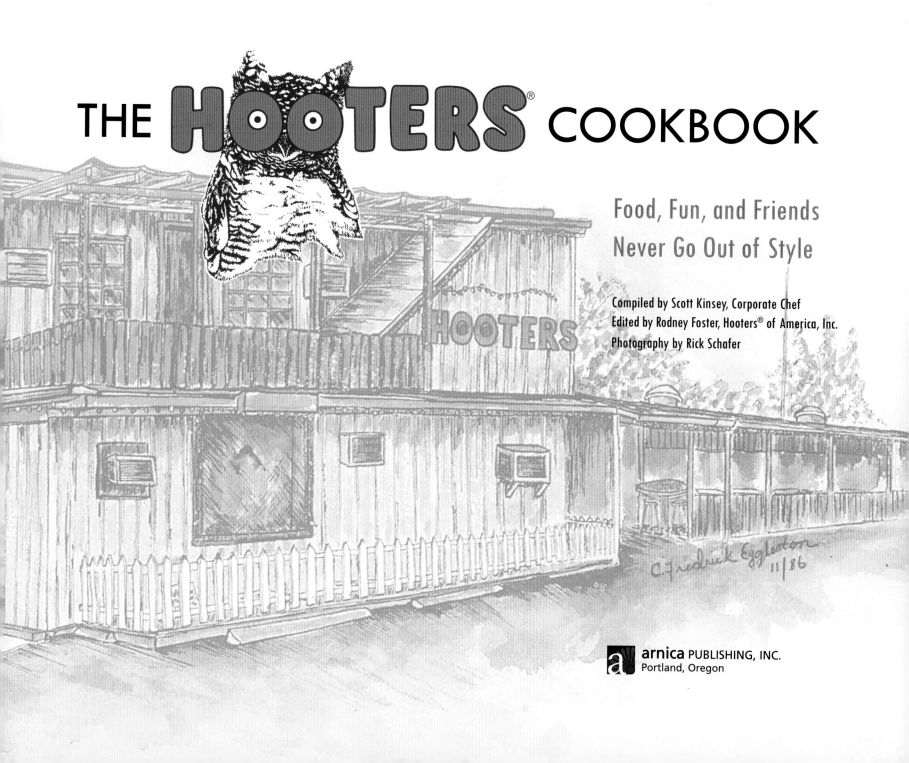

THE HOOTERS COOKBOOK

Food, Fun, and Friends
Never Go Out of Style

Compiled by Scott Kinsey, Corporate Chef
Edited by Rodney Foster, Hooters® of America, Inc.
Photography by Rick Schafer

arnica PUBLISHING, INC.
Portland, Oregon

Library of Congress Cataloging-in-Publication Data
Kinsey, Scott, 1969-
   The Hooters cookbook : food, fun, and friends never go out of style /
compiled by Scott Kinsey ; edited by Rodney Foster ; photographer, Rick
Schafer.
      p. cm.
   ISBN-13: 978-0-9745686-7-6 (alk. paper) 1. Cookery. 2. Hooters
Corporation. I. Foster, Rodney, 1964- II. Hooters Corporation. III. Title.

TX714.K5663 2007
641.5--dc22
                                        2006029308

Special thanks to: Mike McNeil, vice president of
marketing, HOA; Darren Hinerman, publisher,
Hooters® Magazine, and, to Arnica Publishing:
Diane Vines, PhD, board chair, Ross Hawkins, publisher and president, Gloria Gonzalez-Martinez,
vice-president and editor-in-chief; Dick Owsiany,
director of manufacturing; Mattie Ivy, editorial/
production assistant.

Cover and text design by Aimee Genter
Food Photography © Rick Schafer
Food Stylist: Teresa Schafer
All rights reserved, printed in China

Arnica Publishing, Inc.
3739 SE Eighth Ave, Suite 1, Portland, OR 97202
P: (503) 225-9900 F: (503) 225-9901
www.arnicacreative.com

Arnica books are available at special discounts when purchased in bulk for premiums and sales promotions, as well as for fund-raising or educational use.
Special editions or book excerption can also be created for specification. For details, please contact our sales department at the address above.

Dedication

Robert H. Brooks
1933—2006

A Salute to the World Wide Wing Commander

My father was our visionary, leader, friend, and he will be greatly missed. He was an honorable, patriotic, family-oriented Southern gentleman with the courage of a lion—a man who possessed infinite determination, a thoughtful and generous heart, and a drive to fulfill his dreams. He had the unique ability to look out on the horizon and see the next horizon. He was truly a remarkable man.

He was a man who pulled himself up from humble beginnings, overcoming physical adversity and personal tragedy. His struggles sweetened his successes and tempered his resolve through the tough times. Through his many battles, he learned the only way to heal completely is to *give completely*. So he gave, and he made people *happy*. He leaves behind a legacy of generosity that none will ever forget.

He felt passionately about his family, and he loved Hooters®. He never separated his family from his business life. He treated everyone on the Hooters® team as an extension of his own family, and they loved him for that.

His philosophy about Hooters® was simple. He said, "Hooters® makes you happy." His spirit, his vision, and his integrity will continue to be reflected in each and every thing we do as a company as we follow the path of the man who loved to follow the sun, the quiet man in the wings.

Coby G. Brooks, President & CEO,
Hooters® of America, Inc.

v

Table of Contents

Foreword xi

Introduction xiii

Hooters® Through the Ages 1

Wings 6

   Beer-Battered Wings 9

   Buffalo Wings 10

   Waikiki Wings 13

   Asian Chicken Wings 16

   Wings of Fire 19

   Lime Chicken Wings 20

Sandwiches & Burgers 22

   Big Hootie's Burgers 24

   Cali Roll-Ups 27

   Wade's Confetti Salsa 27

   Crab Cake Po' Boys 30

   Yukon Shrimp Hoagies 31

   Stuffed Burgers 33

   More-Than-a-Mouthful Burgers 33

Gameday 34

   Don't Be Crabby Dip 37

   Beer-Crisped Calamari 38

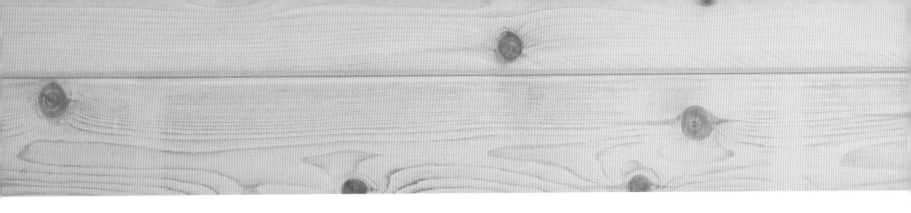

Potato Pigskins 40

Creamy Bean Dip 41

Mini Meatloaves 44

Partychoke Dip 47

Spicy Beer-Battered Onion Rings 48

Brown-Sugar Baked Beans 53

Mama Sue's Chili 54

Sinfully Delicious Bread Bowl 57

Chip's Grits Galore 58

Tailgating & Grilling 60

Fire-in-the-Hole Kabobs 62

Chic-Kabobs 63

Chicken Satay 64

Shrimp on a Stick 66

Roasted Veggie Mishmash 68

Skewers O' Fish 69

Thai Chili Shrimp 72

Tin Man Special 75

Caballero Steak 76

Scotty's Swordfish with Sweet Corn Relish 79

Grilled Steak with Mango Salsa 82

Drunken Chicken 85

Grilled Garden Herb Kabobs 85

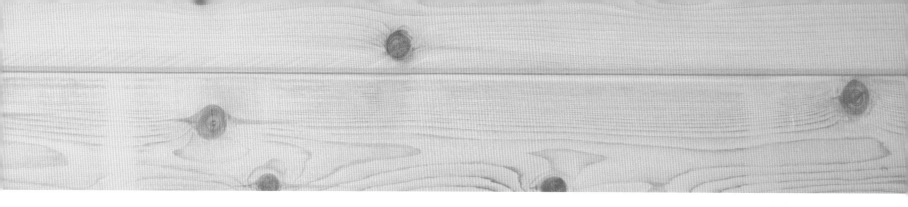

Grilled Mini Poppers 86

Coby's Samurai Rib-Eye 89

Grilled Portobello Mushrooms 89

Recipes to Impress. 90

Coconut Shrimp 93

Creole-Barbecued Oysters 94

Papricot Chicken 97

Cajun-Blackened Halibut 98

Spareribs 101

Cajun Shrimp Bake 104

Spicy Beef and Pepper Jack Quiche 106

Turkey and Cheese Quiche 107

Dungeness Crab Fried Rice 108

Lynne Austin's Lucky 7-Layer Salad 111

Cajun's Choice® Crawfish Boil 112

Dirt Pie 115

Toffee Apple Dip 116

Green Pay Packed Peanut Butter Balls 119

Rockin' Cocktails 120

Iced Tea 122

Hooterberry Lemonade 123

Bleu Hawaiian Salad 125

Caribbean Chicken Salad 125

Foreword

DICK VITALE, college basketball's top analyst, former coach of the NBA's Detroit Pistons, and ESPN.com sports columnist.

Hooters® Fans,

I'll have to admit, in 2000 when I first signed on to the Hooters® team, I was a little reluctant to do so. After some long discussion with my agent and my family, I decided to join the line-up because of Hooters'® commitment to make a sizable donation to the Jimmy V Foundation each year. I have never once regretted that decision.

In the six years that I have been a spokesperson for Hooters®, I have learned to deeply appreciate, respect, and love the Hooters® of America family. My family and I love the food, and the atmosphere is always welcoming and fun. Their unwavering commitment to supporting worthwhile charities such as the Jimmy V Foundation and the Make-A-Wish Foundation is *Awesome, Baby!*

Hooters® is a passionate and dynamic team of players that perform their work with enthusiasm, dedication, and pride. They are always looking for new ways to give back to their communities, to support their employees, and to ensure that the food served in their restaurants meets the expectations of their loyal fans and customers.

There is really nothing better in life than spending quality time among good friends and family. That's what this cookbook is all about. It's the lifestyle that makes Hooters® what it is, and that lifestyle is embodied in these pages: family, friends, and fun is really what it's all about.

This cookbook, a collection of entertaining and tasty recipes gathered from friends and family of Hooters® of America, is a great way to begin creating enduring memories of your own. I gotta say it: *This Hooters® Cookbook is a Dipsy-doo Dunk-a-roo!*

Dick Vitale

Introduction

Dear Friends,

Upon joining the Naturally Fresh® and Hooters® of America family of companies in 1989, I knew from the beginning I had found an everlasting family. Being a very devoted family person, the opportunity to have a chance to develop an extended family away from home was one of the most important decisions of my career. As each one of us strives daily for the proper balance of work, play and family, it is very important we share them in the proper environment.

As I have grown with these companies, it has become more evident each day that food not only touches our lives as a source of nutrition, but that mealtime is the best opportunity to share our experiences and memories with those we love. I think back on my younger years—about all the great times shared with parents and grandparents around the kitchen table, participating together in the preparation of the food or the cleaning chores—these times certainly spawned and nurtured my love for food. It also kindled a life-long dream to be involved with a company that could lend in sharing these great times with family and friends. Whether it is using products from Naturally Fresh®, or enjoying a dining experience at a Hooters® near you, good times are always in store.

While we endured a tremendous loss to our family in July 2006, the passing of our World Wide Wing Commander, many opportunities have also opened up for our extended family to continue to grow from the lessons and values he gave us over the years. Being very fortunate to work alongside such a great man was an extraordinary pleasure. With his guidance, we were always excited to present new ideas and opportunities to the world. From restaurant expansion to new vertical integration, excitement was always around every corner.

Our opportunity to bring this cookbook to you and your family is as exciting as the day we open a new Hooters® location or the day we launched the Hooters® Credit Card. Together, we share our lives in many ways, especially the sharing of great times, tasty food and good friends. We hope you will also find the same excitement each time you prepare one of these recipes from our family—The Hooters® family.

From our table to yours,
Sincerely,

Rodney C. Foster

Rodney C. Foster
Chief Financial Officer, Hooters® of America, Inc.

Hooters® Through the Ages

1983 was a memorable year. Silent film actress Gloria Swanson and pop singer Karen Carpenter both passed away, leaving an admiring America behind. Sally Ride became the first woman to fly in space. And, on one very historic night, six wacky guys in Clearwater, Florida, planned to open a restaurant—one that they couldn't get kicked out of for having "too much fun." They envisioned a place where they could relax, drink some beer, watch some sports, listen to oldies on the juke box, and perhaps most of all, chat with pretty waitresses. These guys had no experience as restaurant managers, but they were expert patrons.

On October 4, 1983, the guys from Clearwater opened the doors to the first Hooters® Restaurant. They offered a menu full of manly food in portions large enough to share, a jukebox loaded with nostalgic 50s and 60s music, and televisions suspended from the ceiling, carrying all the sports a man could watch. *The frosting on the cake?* Hooters® also offered the Hooters® Girls, who were all beautiful, friendly, and entertaining. They were also all female.

Lynne Austin was the first Hooters® Girl, and legend has it that she became so as the result of a spur-of-the-moment bet. While watching a José Cuervo bikini contest from a boat anchored just off Clearwater Beach, Ed Droste, one of the original Hooters® Six, bet his buddies that he could convince the winner of the contest to become the first Hooters® Girl. Droste pitched his offer to Lynne after she won the contest, but she didn't join the team that day. After a few weeks however, she decided working for Hooters® just might be a hoot. That spontaneous bet, placed nearly a quarter-century ago, launched a very successful restaurant chain venture, and today Hooters®

Restaurants are continually opening all over the country and across the globe. And, thanks to Lynne paving the way, the Hooters® Girls alumni now number in the hundreds of thousands.

In 1986, the Hooters® Six sold their restaurant chain to business-savvy Robert H. Brooks, who had already made a name for himself as the owner of Naturally Fresh® Foods. His remarkable leadership helped Hooters® Restaurants to thrive. And his uncanny deal-making skills, family-oriented corporate philosophy, and sharp-minded business sense quickly caught the attention of serious businessmen around the world. As a salute to Brooks' skills, *Fortune Magazine* gave Hooters® serious accolades in a 2003 headline that read: "HOOTERS®: A CASE STUDY 'THIS THING HAS INCREDIBLE LEGS,' AN EARLY INVESTOR SAID. TWENTY YEARS LATER, THE RESTAURANT CHAIN HAS FINALLY HIT ITS STRIDE."

Over the years, the company has maintained its integrity by remaining faithful to the original concept. They fought a long and difficult battle to defend their right to hire only women as food servers, and they have successfully made a name for themselves among the "big guys." Their commitment to service and quality has made Hooters® what it is today. Perhaps the best description of a Hooters® Neighborhood Restaurant comes from the World Wide Wing Commander himself:

"It's someplace to come in, sit down, have a beer...enjoy yourself. All we want to do is take care of the customer and make people happy. There isn't enough happiness in the world."

—ROBERT H. BROOKS, 2003

The Original Hooters® Girl

The original Hooters® Girl, Lynn Austin, was an outgoing bikini-clad beauty with a spunky attitude. She was daring and sultry, as well as naturally friendly, witty, and highly approachable. When her supervisors at GTE decided they couldn't give her time off to attend a bikini contest, she abruptly quit her job and joined the soon-to-be-famous Hooters® Six as they prepared to open the first Hooters® in Clearwater, Florida.

Inspired by the image of Lynne, they developed a simple uniform consisting of short orange jogging shorts, a white tank-top, nylons, white socks and white tennis shoes. The description of a Hooters® Girl, "The All-American Cheerleader Surfer Girl next door" fit Lynne to a T.

Lynn was initiated into the new venture by being given the task of cleaning the refrigerator and scrubbing the floors. Although the beginning was a little less-than-glamorous, Lynn has enjoyed a long-standing career with Hooters®, and, in 1986, was chosen as Playboy Magazine's Playmate of the Month. She was shown wearing her Hooters® Girl uniform...and a lot less. Lynne appeared in dozens of Hooters® TV commercials through the year and was a mainstay of the Hooters® calendar for the first decade. While hundreds of thousands of young women have followed in her footsteps, Lynne will always be the first. She has become a Hooters® icon.

Austin, who remains under a personal services contract with Hooters®, now co-hosts an all-female sports talk radio show known as *Sportschix*, in the Tampa Bay, Florida area. She still looks great and says of her Hooters® Girl experience, "It's been a helluva ride!"

Alan Kulwicki

Hooters® has an unusual style of seizing unlikely opportunities and creating seem-ingly befuddling relationships that tend to have the business community scratching their heads in confusion while simultaneously applauding the untamed creativity and pioneering spirit that have given Hooters® their unparalleled personality.

In 1991, Hooters® cut a deal with the up-and-coming owner/driver Alan Kulwicki, to sponsor his car for a NASCAR race in Atlanta. That one-event deal blossomed into full season Hooters® sponsorship for Kulwicki in 1992, and the little underdog, nicknamed "Mighty Mouse," won the presti-gious NASCAR Winston Cup Championship at the last race of the season that fittingly was the Hooters® 500 which happened to be in Atlanta on the very track where it had all started with Hooters®. It has since become tradition for winners of this event to duplicate his patented reverse "Polish victory lap" every year.

Kelly Jo Dowd

In 2002, Kelly Jo Dowd, a former Hooters® Calendar Girl, was diagnosed with breast cancer after discovering a lump during a routine breast self-examination. Upon hearing the news, Hooters® of America rallied behind Kelly Jo in her valiant battle against this quiet killer. Unfortunately, in 2004, after the battle was thought to be over, Kelly's cancer returned. Today, she fights stage IV metastasized breast cancer. To team up with Kelly Jo, and to express their commitment to improving the odds for the 1 in 7 Hooters® Girls who will develop breast cancer in their lifetimes, Hooters® of America has pledged a $1 million breast cancer research grant in her name. Our efforts to help Kelly Jo with her struggle is just one example of how we hope to make a difference.

Photo © David Yellen

Kelly Jo and her daughter, Dakoda Dowd, who was awarded a coveted sponsor's exemption at the age of 13 in an LPGA Tour event. The offer was in response to her mother's public wish to see her daughter play on the LPGA tour. "I wasn't going to fight when I learned the cancer had returned. I'd gotten depressed but, when I had gotten to my lowest point, I found the strength in my daughter's eyes and in her heart," explained Kelly Jo.

Mourning Our Champions

Tragically, on April 1, 1993, while on a promotional trip, Robert H. Brooks' son, Mark Brooks, Dan Duncan, Charlie Campbell, and fan-favorite Alan Kulwicki all perished when their plan crashed just outside of Bristol, TN.

When asked about the terrible accident, Robert Brooks said, "It hurt me more than anything." Out of his deep personal grief he developed a profound resolution to memorialize his son and the other three fallen champions. He campaigned to have the USAR Hooters® Pro Cup Four Champions Series named after them, and he worked to establish the Hooters® Memorial Cup Golf Tournament as a way to memorialize them. Since 1993, over $2 million has been raised by events such as the Hooters® Memorial Cup Golf Tournament for The Hooters® Community Endowment Fund.

As a tribute to the fallen champions, proceeds from the Hooters® Memorial Cup Golf Tournament have aided in creating the Brooks Motorsports Institute, which has provided Clemson University with the country's best interdisciplinary program for the study of the motorsports industry.

"Mr. Brooks' philanthropy fundamentally changed Clemson University's definitions of quality, sophistication, artistic excellence and outreach," said Lillian Harder, director of the Clemson University performing arts center that bears Brooks' name.

Hooters® "Independence Day"

In 1991, the Equal Employment Opportunity Commission (EEOC) filed a commissioner's charge against Hooters®, alleging that the company's hiring practices were discriminatory against men, and challenging Hooters®' right to hire only women as Hooters® Girls.

After four years of costly investigation and ridiculous documentation requests by the EEOC, the agency concluded that Hooters® should, along with a slew of other sanctions that would have effectively put Hooters® out of business, hire men to be Hooters® Girls. Rather than accept the EEOC's offer, Hooters® decided to fight back. They launched an eye-popping public awareness plan that ignited a grass-roots response and stunned the entire nation, including Congress.

On November 15, 1995, during a press conference held during the famous Hooters® Girls March in Washington, Hooters® ushered into world view Vince, "The Hooters® Guy." Not wanting their new spokesman to go unnoticed, the company plastered larger-than-life images of the buxom, hairy, mustachioed Vince, proudly wearing his Hooters® Girl uniform throughout major newspapers, strategically placed billboards, and 150 million television screens carried the message: "Hooters® Guys? Washington, Get a Grip."

The public outcry was overwhelming. Phone calls and letters from taxpayers who supported the Hooters® concept flooded Congress and the offices of the EEOC. Why, the taxpayers demanded, was the EEOC, with a 100,000-case backlog, spending so much time and federal money fighting a restaurant chain simply for providing the brilliant combination of good food, cold beer, and pretty girls?

The public awareness plan, obviously, had worked, and in May of 1996, Hooters® received word that the EEOC would cease efforts to re-gender the Hooters® Girl. In honor of this freedom, November 15, 1995 will always be known as Hooters® Independence Day!

What could have been...

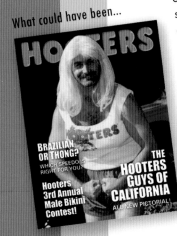

Get what you've always wanted at Hooters®: free food. Hooters® has introduced the Hooters® Credit Card to reward regulars like you with extra points for every dollar you spend at Hooters®.

The first edition of Hooters® Magazine came out in Winter 1989.

The first newsstand issue hit the streets in September 2005.

Operation: Let Freedom Wing

Let Freedom Wing... Tank You.

Hooters® of America is passionate about communicating to our troops that the country deeply appreciates their personal sacrifice, and we actively support the troops overseas by sponsoring a variety of nationwide promotions. Take, for example, Operation Calendar Drop, a yearly campaign that enables our customers to send Hooters® calendars, signed by our Hooters® Girls and sealed by our managers, to more than 20,000 service personnel who spend the holidays in less-than-desirable conditions.

As another example of how we have worked to boost the troops' morale, in May of 2004, Hooters® sent out the Hooters® Calendar Girls and their all-girl singing group, UC3, on an Armed Forces Entertainment tour through the Middle East and Afghanistan. The response from soldiers who attended the tour, dubbed "Operation: Let Freedom Wing," was overwhelming. We received countless letters from soldiers thanking our stores and customers for the support they received during that tour.

Further examples of how we support the troops throughout the year include our Hooters® Salutes feature, which appears in each issue of Hooters® magazine, and Hooters® "Care Packages," which we send monthly to soldiers serving in harm's way.

HOO.C.E.F.
Hooters® Community Endowment Fund: Giving Something Back

Community involvement has always been a cornerstone of the Hooters® concept. In 1992, Hooters® of America established the Hooters® Community Endowment Fund (HOO.C.E.F.), a 501-C(3) nonprofit organization, intended to centralize monies raised by individual stores and specific fundraising activities and give them back to the communities we serve.

HOO.C.E.F. has since provided millions of dollars to support such charitable causes as the American Red Cross, the V Foundation for Cancer Research, the Make-A-Wish Foundation, Special Olympics, the Muscular Dystrophy Association, and the Juvenile Diabetes Foundation. It is not unusual to see the Hooters® Girls cheerfully hosting charity events or car washes to make a difference in the lives of others.

WINGS

Wing-eating is a bonding experience, according to aficionados of the art. It brings out the best and the worst in people. Eating with your hands makes you feel like a kid again, if only because there's always sauce on your fingers and there's no fun in using a napkin.

For those of you who don't know the ins and outs of a chicken wing, here are a few must-know terms:

- **Wing Tip or Nub:** the part of the chicken wing that is usually removed before cooking. Hooters® serves wings with tips for a little extra bite.
- **Drum or Drummie:** the part of the wing that looks like a drumstick.
- **"Boneless" Wings:** This is the version of wings that the yuppies eat. (We recommend approaching this type of wing with caution—if there are no bones, how can it fly?)

Beer-Battered Wings

Hooters® wings come in quantities of 10, 20, and 50. And if you're feeling fancy, try the Hooters® Gourmet Chicken Wing Dinner. It's 20 wings and a bottle of Korbel champagne.

For those who need a wing-fix but don't like to shop, here's a recipe you can make in minutes with ingredients you have around the house. If you don't have any pale ale, any old beer will do, even those warm ones under the couch.

What you'll need:

18 whole chicken wings
Vegetable oil, for frying
Your favorite barbecue or dipping sauce
Paper towels

For the beer batter:
1 cup flour
1/4 cup cornstarch
1 cup pale ale
Pinch of salt
1 tablespoon freshly ground black pepper

What to do:

To make the beer batter, combine the flour, cornstarch, pale ale, salt, and pepper. Whisk these ingredients together and refrigerate until ready to use.

Cut the chicken wings into three sections and discard the wing tips. Dip the wings in the batter and deep-fry until golden brown. Drain on a paper towel and serve with your favorite barbecue or dipping sauce.

Yield: 3 servings

Tip for the lazy boy:

Make a beeline to your nearest Hooters® and pick up some wings! *(Have your choice of Mild, Medium, Hot, 3 Mile island, 911, Samurai, and Cajun.)*

9

Buffalo Wings

Vice President Mondale had buffalo wings delivered to his plane on a visit to Buffalo, NY, as did the former First Lady, Hillary Clinton. (Although it's rumored her husband just went to Hooters®.)

What you'll need:

18 chicken wings
6 tablespoons butter or margarine
1/4 cup hot red pepper sauce
Vegetable oil, for frying
Bleu cheese dressing, for dipping
Paper towels

What to do:

Cut the chicken wings into three sections and discard the wing tips.

Melt the butter in a small sauce pan. Add the hot sauce and remove from heat. Set aside.

Heat 1 inch of oil in a large frying pan or deep-fat fryer to 360°F. Fry the wings in batches, without crowding them, for about 10 to 15 minutes, or until golden brown. Drain on paper towels. Brush the wings with the spicy butter mixture and serve warm with bleu cheese dressing for dipping.

Yield: 3 servings

Oh, give me a home...

Where the Buffalo Wings roam

Where the wings and the spicy sauce mix.

Where seldom is heard a discouraging word

And they make you look good to the chicks.

Waikiki Wings

All the fun of the beach without the sand in your drawers. Proclaim yourself the Big Kahuna with these easy-to-make island treats. Sweet and salty, they'll satisfy any craving.

What you'll need:

18 whole chicken wings
1 1/2 cups finely chopped fresh pineapple
3/4 cup prepared barbecue sauce
1 tablespoon soy sauce
1/2 teaspoon ground ginger
Pineapple wedges, for garnish

What to do:

Cut the chicken wings into three sections and discard the wing tips.

Combine the chopped pineapple, barbecue sauce, soy sauce, and ginger in a 9 by 13-inch glass baking dish. Add the chicken and coat on all sides with the sauce. Cover and marinate for 15 minutes in the fridge.

Grill or broil the chicken for 15 to 20 minutes, or until the chicken is no longer pink, brushing occasionally with marinade and turning once halfway through cooking. Discard the remaining marinade. Garnish with pineapple wedges if desired.

Yield: 3 servings

FOOTBALL

We've noticed a strange phenomenon as we watch those of you who come into Hooters® to watch the game... you do some weird things with your wings:

WINGY ROULETTE: This game is a great one for playing while watching the half-time show. It is a high-stakes game of chance. Begin with a ten-piece order of mild Hooters® wings. Order another with Three-Mile Island sauce, and mix the two wing choices together. Randomly pick wings out of the mix, and the wing-eater who gets the highest number of super-hot wings supplies the next round of beer and wings. This can continue throughout the night, tournament style.

WINGA: This game is played just like the popular table game, Jenga®. The competition begins by stacking discarded wings on top of each other on a small "wing plate." This is where the game differs slightly from the original. In Winga, whoever places the wing that causes the growing stack to fall to the table loses the game and must provide the next round of beer and wings. This also can continue throughout the day, tournament-style.

Personal Foul

Offside

Timeout

Touchdown or Field Goal

KNOW the SIGNS

Yeah, you know the signs. You've known them since you were in diapers. But the next time your wife, girlfriend or mother asks, "What does it mean when the guy in the stripey shirt puts his hands on his hips?" just show her this page. The hard part will be explaining what "offside" means.

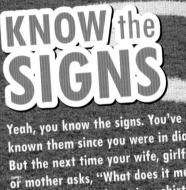

Interference with a forward pass

Too many men on the field

First down

Holding

15

Asian Chicken Wings

It would take 15 hours to fly from Hooters®
Headquarters in Atlanta, Georgia to Tokyo, Japan.

What you'll need:

18 chicken wings
2/3 cup water
2/3 cup soy sauce
6 tablespoons packed brown sugar
3 tablespoons dry sherry
3 teaspoons finely minced fresh ginger
Sesame seeds, to taste

What to do:

Cut the chicken wings into three sections and discard the wing tips. Combine the water, soy sauce, brown sugar, sherry, and ginger in a large cooking pot and bring to a boil. Reduce the heat, cover, and simmer for 20 minutes, stirring occasionally. Uncover the pot, increase the heat slightly and continue cooking, stirring often, for another 15 minutes, or until the sauce has become a rich, thick glaze.

Preheat the oven to 350°F. Place the wings into a glass baking dish and bake for 45 minutes. When the wings are done baking, toss them in the sauce to thoroughly coat. Garnish with sesame seeds.

Serve hot or cold.

Yield: 3 servings

Travel east—far east—without leaving the comforts of home. The aroma of fresh ginger will transport you to the land of many happy delights. No need for chopsticks; you can eat 'em with your hands.

Wings of Fire

Picante is a Spanish adjective that derives from *picar*, which means "to sting," referring to the feeling caused by hot peppers on one's tongue.

Legend has it, the Devil himself won't touch these wings without a bucket of ice nearby. Not spicy enough for ya? Add some crushed red pepper flakes. And for the less adventurous, there's no shame in cutting down on the chipotle sauce.

What you'll need:

18 whole chicken wings
1/2 teaspoon salt
1/8 teaspoon freshly ground
    black pepper
2 tablespoons vegetable oil
1/2 cup butter, divided in half
1/2 cup red or green mild taco
    sauce
1/4 cup prepared barbecue
    sauce

1/4 cup French dressing
1 teaspoon Worcestershire
    sauce
1/2 teaspoon chipotle sauce
Tabasco sauce
Oil or shortening, for greasing
    the baking pan

What to do:

Cut the chicken wings into three sections and discard the wing tips. Sprinkle the wings with salt and pepper.

Combine the vegetable oil and half of the butter, and fry the chicken in a skillet over medium heat until brown. Place the wings in a greased 9 by 13-inch baking pan.

Combine the taco sauce, barbecue sauce, French dressing, Worcestershire sauce, chipotle sauce, and the remaining butter in a sauce pan, cook and stir over medium heat until the butter is melted and the sauce is blended. Pour a 1/2 cup of the sauce over the chicken wings, reserving some sauce for later.

Preheat the oven to 300° F. Bake the wings uncovered for 15 to 20 minutes. Serve with the remaining sauce and/or Tabasco sauce to taste.

Yield: 3 servings

19

Lime Chicken Wings

It's a tough life for a lime. It's not easy being lonely and green. But when a lime teams up with a chicken—watch out!— you're in for a lime-y, tangy, wingy surprise.

Competitive eating is a coed sport. Sonya Thomas, a 105-pound woman from Virginia holds the current chicken wing-eating record, having gobbled up 167 wings in 32 minutes! That eats the wings off of 83.5 chickens!

What you'll need:

18 whole chicken wings
1 cup ketchup
1/4 cup freshly squeezed lime juice
2 tablespoons liquid smoke
1 tablespoon Worcestershire sauce
1 tablespoon balsamic vinegar
2 tablespoons brown sugar
1 teaspoon hot pepper sauce
1 teaspoon granulated garlic powder
1/4 cup minced sweet onion

Plan Ahead Alert! The wings need to marinate in the fridge overnight before cooking.

What to do:

Cut the chicken wings into three sections and discard the wing tips.

Combine the ketchup, lime juice, liquid smoke, Worcestershire sauce, vinegar, brown sugar, hot pepper sauce, garlic powder, and sweet onion in a mixing bowl. Place the chicken wings in a shallow glass dish, pour in the lime mixture, cover, and refrigerate overnight.

Fire up the grill, and cook for about 20 minutes, basting and turning occasionally.

Yield: 3 servings

& BURGERS

The basic sandwich is the perfect meal for the busy modern American. It's simple. It's satisfying. It's portable. But the sandwich has actually been around for hundreds of years. For example, Middle Eastern countries have been filling pita bread with lamb and veggies long before we started calling them "sandwiches."

The popularity of the sandwich in American culture is evident. We eat 300 million sandwiches each day—that's more than one for every man, woman and child in the nation!

Big Hootie's Burgers

Each month, Hooters® uses over 50,000 pounds of ground beef. That's 600,000 pounds a year, which adds up to the same weight as 1,000 motorcycles or 120 hippopotamuses!

What you'll need:

1 tablespoon olive oil
1 onion, chopped
4 cloves garlic, minced
4 tablespoons Worcestershire sauce
4 slices bacon, crisp-cooked and crumbled
1 large egg, beaten

1/2 tablespoon salt
1/4 teaspoon freshly ground black pepper
1/4 tablespoon hot pepper sauce
2 pounds ground beef chuck
4 slices Cheddar cheese
4 of your favorite large rolls

What to do:

Heat the oil in a nonstick skillet over medium heat. Add the onions and garlic, and sauté until brown and thoroughly cooked, about 8 minutes. Transfer the sautéed onions and garlic to a bowl. Mix in the Worcestershire sauce, bacon, egg, salt, pepper, and hot pepper sauce. Add the beef and combine by hand or with a wooden spoon until evenly blended.

Form the mixture into 4 large patties. Reheat the skillet to medium-high heat. Add the patties and cook for 5 minutes. Flip the patties and top each with a slice of cheese. Cook to desired doneness.

Serve on rolls with your favorite condiments.

Yield: 4 servings

Juicy, spicy, big and bacon-y,

a cacophony of flavor for you to savor.

Add some ranch to cool it down, or throw

in some jalapeños to make it spicy.

Cali Roll-Ups

California knows how to party.
With Cali Roll-Ups, the party comes to you.

What you'll need:

1 cup refried black beans
4 10-inch whole-wheat tortillas
1 cup shredded Cheddar cheese
2 ripe avocados, sliced
1 red onion, thinly sliced
1 16-ounce jar chunky-style salsa
2 cups alfalfa sprouts

What to do:

Heat the refried beans in the microwave for 1 minute. Lay the tortillas out on the counter. Spread the refried beans evenly over each tortilla. Sprinkle each tortilla with the cheese. Arrange the avocado and onion slices over the cheese. Spread the salsa over the onions and avocado. Sprinkle the sprouts on top of the salsa. Roll up the tortilla, beginning at one edge and folding the open ends inward as you roll. Cut the tortilla roll diagonally into 4 equal parts and serve.

Yield: 4 servings

Wade's Confetti Salsa

What you'll need:

4 tomatoes	2 jalapeño peppers
2 sweet white onions	1 lime
2 green bell peppers	2 tablespoons hot sauce
2 yellow bell peppers	1 tablespoon adobo seasoning
2 red bell peppers	1 tablespoon cracked black
1 bunch cilantro	pepper
3 mangoes	Tortilla chips

What to do:

Thoroughly wash all of the vegetables. Core the tomatoes and cut them in half. Remove the guts and seeds from the tomatoes and discard. Dice the rinds into small pieces, and place them in a large bowl. Peel and dice the onions and place them into the bowl along with the tomatoes. Core and de-seed the bell peppers. Dice them and put them in the bowl with the tomatoes and onions.

Peel the mangoes, remove their cores, and dice them into small pieces. Put them into the mixing bowl. De-seed the jalapeños and add the seeds to the bowl. Dice the chiles and add them to the bowl. Finally, mince the cilantro and add it to the bowl. Toss together all the veggies in the bowl.

Squeeze the lime over the diced veggies. Add the hot sauce, adobo seasoning, and black pepper, and mix well. Refrigerate for one hour and serve with tortilla chips.

Yield: A large bowl of Confetti Salsa...*Duh!*

GOLF

The NGA/Hooters Tour, which puts a greater emphasis on strong community support, well-organized events, and benefiting local charities, has helped more professionals acquire their PGA, Senior PGA, and Nationwide Tour cards than any other developmental tour. With professionalism a focal point of this tour, the golf community and corporate America continue to be attracted to the high visibility and unique exposure opportunities presented by the NGA/Hooters Professional Golf Tour.

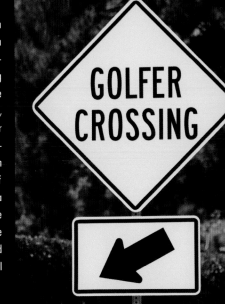

The all-time wins and money leader on the NGA Hooters Pro Golf Tour is Chad Campbell, with 13 wins and $776,976 in earnings.

There are 336 dimples on a regulation golf ball.

Dimples on a golf ball reduce drag by creating turbulence as the ball flies through the air.

Early shepherds may have used their curved staffs to hit stones in a simple game of "golf" as early as 2,000 years ago.

A more structured version of golf was invented in Scotland nearly 1,000 years ago.

The first golf balls were made of thin leather stuffed with feathers. Tightly-packed feathers made balls that flew the farthest. Feather balls were used until 1848.

The youngest golfer to shoot a hole-in-one was Coby Orr, who was five years old at the time. It happened in Littleton, Colorado, in 1975.

Posted at a Local Golf Club:

1. Back straight, knees bent, feet shoulder-width apart.
2. Form a loose grip.
3. Keep your head down.
4. Avoid a quick back swing.
5. Stay out of the water.
6. Try not to hit anyone.
7. If you are taking too long, please let others go ahead of you.
8. Don't stand directly in front of others.
9. Quiet please while others are preparing to go.
10. Don't take extra strokes.

Very good. Now flush, go outside, and tee off.

It's all in the NAME

1. Who is nicknamed Fuzzy?
2. What golfer obtained the nickname of Montie?
3. Lefty is the obvious nickname of...?
4. Fluff is the strange nickname of whom?
5. The Squire was the nickname of what golfer?
6. Who earned the nickname of Boom-Boom?
7. The Walrus is the nickname of what famous golfer?
8. Tiger is the famous nickname of what professional golfer?
9. What golfer has the nickname of Lumpy?
10. El Niño is the nickname of what golfer?
11. What golfer earned the name Squeeky?
12. Slammin' Sammy is the nickname of what professional golfer?
13. The nickname, the Great White Shark, is associated with which golfer?
14. Chi Chi is the nickname of whom?
15. Golden Bear is the famous nickname of what golfer?
16. Which pro golfer's nickname is The Lion?

1. Frank Zoeller.
2. Colin Montgomerie.
3. Phil Mickelson.
4. Mike Cowan.
5. Gene Sarazen.
6. Fred Couples.
7. Craig Stadler.
8. Eldrick Woods.
9. Tim Herron.
10. Sergio Garcia.
11. Jeff Medlen.
12. Sam Snead.
13. Greg Norman.
14. Juan Rodriguez.
15. Jack Nicklaus.
16. John Daly.

Crab Cake Po' Boys

These po' boys won't be asking you for spare change; they're rich enough already. Rich in flavor, that is.

What you'll need:

For the po' boy:
6 French rolls
1 tablespoon finely chopped parsley, tarragon, and thyme, blended
1 cup bread crumbs
12 ounces lump crab meat, drained
1 cup flour
Vegetable oil, for frying
Tomatoes, thinly sliced
Lettuce leaves, washed and dried

For the Rémoulade Sauce:
2 tablespoons chopped jarred capers
2 cups of your favorite tartar sauce
2 teaspoons Cajun seasoning
1 teaspoon prepared horseradish
6 dashes Tabasco or other hot pepper sauce, for flavor

What to do:

Preparing the po' boy:
Preheat the oven to 375°F. Split the rolls in half lengthwise, leaving a hinge along one side. Hollow out the center of the top and the bottom of each roll. Place the bread crumbs and herb mixture in a blender and whir to make about 1 cup of fine crumbs. Set aside.

Add the crab meat and 1 cup of the Rémoulade Sauce in a medium bowl. Stir gently. Add the breadcrumb mixture and lightly toss until just combined. Form 12 crab cakes, about 2 1/2 inches in diameter. Pour the flour onto a pie plate or other shallow dish. Carefully coat the crab cakes with the flour, and set aside.

Heat oil to medium-high heat and fry the crab cakes in batches until they are golden brown, about 2 minutes per side. Transfer to a sheet pan, and bake the crab cakes in the preheated oven for 8 to 10 minutes.

Serve the crab cakes on hollowed-out French rolls with lettuce, tomato, and additional Rémoulade sauce.

Preparing the Rémoulade Sauce:
Mash the capers with a fork in a small bowl. Add in the tartar sauce, Cajun seasoning, horseradish, and hot pepper sauce, and mix well. Chill in the refrigerator (if time permits), covered, for at least 1 hour.

Yield: 6 servings

Yukon Shrimp Hoagie

What do you get when you mix shrimp, beer, and bread?
One heckuva tasty sandwich, that's what.

What you'll need:

2 quarts water
7 cloves garlic
3 bay leaves
2 tablespoons Old Bay® seasoning
3 lemon slices
2 tablespoons salt
12 ounces dark lager
2 pounds medium shrimp, shells and
    tails attached

12 ice cubes
4 hoagie rolls
Your favorite dipping sauce

Optional:
1 lettuce leaf per hoagie
1 or 2 slices of tomato per hoagie

What to do:

Combine the water, garlic, bay leaves, Old Bay® seasoning, lemon slices, and salt into a 1-gallon stockpot, and bring to a boil. Add the dark lager and the shrimp once the water has reached a rolling boil. Stir well and cook for a few minutes until the shells turn pink.

Pour the ice cubes into a large metal bowl. Remove the shrimp from the boiling water with a slotted spoon, and place them into the ice. Wait for the shrimp to cool, then remove the shells and tails. Place the shrimp onto the hoagie rolls with your favorite dipping sauce. Add lettuce and tomato, if you choose.

Yield: 4 servings

Stuffed Burgers

What you'll need:

For the filling:
4 bacon slices, crisp-cooked and crumbled
2 ounces crumbled bleu cheese
2 teaspoons chopped, fresh oregano

For the burger:
2 1/2 pounds ground beef
3 tablespoons blackening seasoning

1 large red onion, sliced 1/4-inch-thick slices
Olive oil, as needed
6 hamburger buns
Mayonnaise
6 lettuce leaves
6 tomato slices

What to do:

Mix the bacon, cheese, and oregano together in a bowl and set aside. Place the ground beef in a large mixing bowl and add the blackening seasoning. Mix well by hand. Divide the beef into 6 separate portions and shape each into a ball. Make a depression in each ball with your thumb. Spoon about 1 tablespoon of the bacon-bleu cheese filling into the depressions of each ball. Shape the meat gently around the filling until the filling is completely sealed. Press the balls into patties, making sure they are about 1-inch thick. Place the patties on a cookie sheet and set aside.

Place the onion slices into a small mixing bowl with enough olive oil to coat them completely. Toss with your hands to ensure they are well coated.

Fire up the grill. Lay the onion rings flat on the grill, making sure that they do not fall through the gaps. Grill for 10 to 12 minutes, turning every 4 minutes or so, until the onions start to caramelize. Remove from grill and set aside. Grill the burgers to desired doneness. Transfer each burger to a bun after spreading mayo on the top half. Top each burger with grilled onion slices, lettuce, and tomatoes.

Yield: 6 servings

More-Than-a-Mouthful Burgers

What you'll need:

3 pounds ground sirloin
1 pound ground sausage
1 pound bacon, crisp-cooked and crumbled
1 egg
8 ounces shredded mozzarella cheese
8 ounces shredded Cheddar cheese
8 ounces shredded pepper Jack cheese

8 ounces colby Jack cheese, cut into 1/2-inch cubes
1 small white onion, minced
2 tablespoons chili powder
2 teaspoons salt
2 teaspoons freshly ground black pepper
6 hamburger buns
Butter, for toasting the buns

What to do:

Combine the sirloin, sausage, bacon, egg, mozzarella, Cheddar, pepper Jack, colby Jack, onion, chili powder, salt, and pepper in a large mixing bowl. Mash the mixture up well with your hands, making sure that the cubed colby Jack stays cubed. Form into patties. Refrigerate, if prepared ahead of time, separating the patties with wax paper.

Fire up the grill, and throw on the burgers. Toast the buns a few minutes before the burgers are ready by brushing them with butter and grilling them butter-side down. When browned, load the buns with the burgers and eat. Repeat as necessary for desired fullness.

Yield: 6 burgers

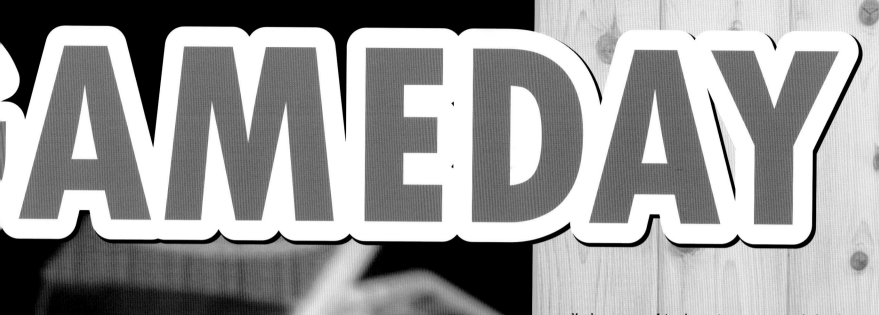

GAMEDAY

You've got your friends coming over to watch the play-offs. There's only $9.54 in your checking account, and your laundry hasn't been done in 3 weeks. Your dishes have gone past moldy and slimy to the petrified, unidentifiable stage, and you only have five hot dogs and a can of chili in your kitchen. You ask yourself:

"What Would Hooters® Do?"

The answer is simple. All you have to do is turn the page for some great, quick-and-easy recipes that will work for the occasion. Now, about the laundry and dishes... well, you're on your own with those.

"Don't Be Crabby" Dip

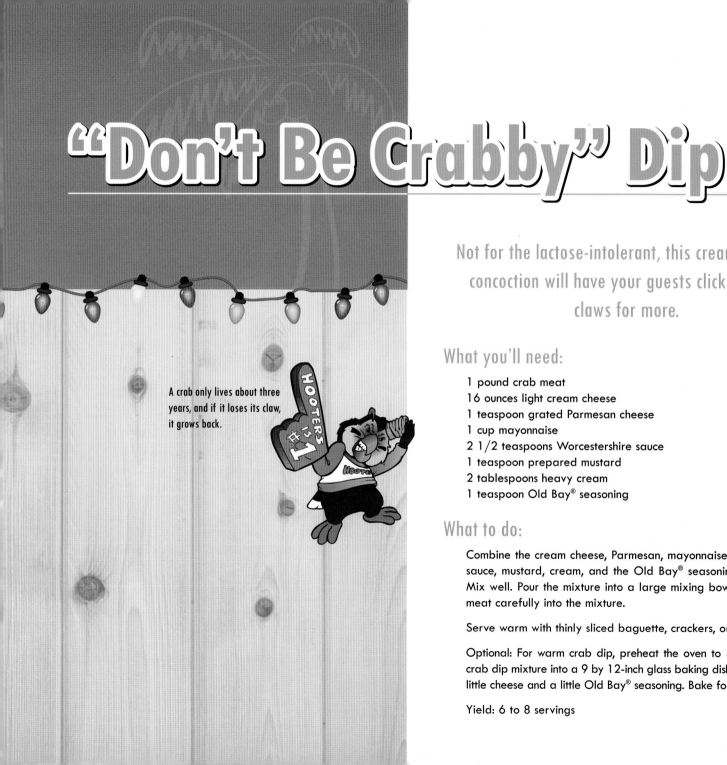

A crab only lives about three years, and if it loses its claw, it grows back.

Not for the lactose-intolerant, this creamy, crabby concoction will have your guests clicking their claws for more.

What you'll need:

1 pound crab meat
16 ounces light cream cheese
1 teaspoon grated Parmesan cheese
1 cup mayonnaise
2 1/2 teaspoons Worcestershire sauce
1 teaspoon prepared mustard
2 tablespoons heavy cream
1 teaspoon Old Bay® seasoning

What to do:

Combine the cream cheese, Parmesan, mayonnaise, Worcestershire sauce, mustard, cream, and the Old Bay® seasoning in a blender. Mix well. Pour the mixture into a large mixing bowl. Fold the crab meat carefully into the mixture.

Serve warm with thinly sliced baguette, crackers, or pita chips.

Optional: For warm crab dip, preheat the oven to 325°F. Place the crab dip mixture into a 9 by 12-inch glass baking dish. Sprinkle with a little cheese and a little Old Bay® seasoning. Bake for 30 minutes.

Yield: 6 to 8 servings

37

Beer-Crisped Calamari

It's a fact that the giant squid can grow up to 45 feet long. Don't risk it! Eat them before they get big enough to eat you.

Paprika comes from dried and ground chile peppers, *capsicum annuum*, which originated in southern Mexico. Capsicum is a member of the nightshade family, which also includes potatoes and tomatoes.

What you'll need:

2 pounds frozen, sliced squid rings
1 12-ounce light beer
1/2 cup peanut oil
1 1/2 cup vegetable oil
1 cup flour
1 teaspoon salt
1/2 teaspoon freshly ground black pepper
2 tablespoons paprika
Tartar sauce (or your favorite dipping sauce)
Paper towels

Plan Ahead Alert! This recipe requires thawing the squid overnight.

What to do:

Rinse the frozen squid rings to remove any excess ice chunks, and place them in a large, zippered freezer bag. Pour the beer into the bag, zip it up, and let the squid thaw in the refrigerator overnight.

When the squid is thawed, combine the peanut and vegetable oils in a large, deep, heavy skillet, and heat to frying temperature (about medium-high). Combine the flour, salt, pepper, and paprika in a large mixing bowl. Mix well with a whisk. Drop the squid rings into the mixture and coat thoroughly.

Place 8 to 10 coated squid rings into the hot oil, and fry for about 45 seconds, or until golden brown. Repeat as necessary until all squid rings have been fried. Drain the fried calamari on paper towels and serve with tartar sauce.

Yield: 4 to 6 servings

Potato Pigskins

What you'll need:

3 pounds red creamer potatoes, scrubbed

3 cups prepared ranch dressing

4 boiled eggs, chopped

3 ounces (1 jar) bacon bits

1 stalk celery, sliced

2 cups shredded Cheddar cheese

4 scallions, sliced

Fresh baby chives, chopped

1 teaspoon paprika

Salt, to taste

Freshly ground black pepper, to taste

24 slices of deli-style ham (or favorite lunch meat)

What to do:

Place the washed potatoes in a large pot and cover with water. Bring to a rolling boil, reduce heat, and simmer until easily poked with a knife, approximately 20 to 30 minutes. Drain the potatoes and let cool. Dice the potatoes and place them in a large bowl. Toss them with the ranch dressing, eggs, bacon bits, celery, cheese, scallions, chives, and paprika. Sprinkle with salt and freshly ground black pepper, to taste.

Put two spoonfuls of potato salad on each slice of ham and roll it up into a funnel. Eat right away or refrigerate for the big game.

Yield: 6 to 8 hungry sports fans

Tips for the lazy boy:

Forget the entire first paragraph of the instructions. Get a bucket of potato salad and some lunch meat at the store. Spoon it. Roll it. Eat it.

It's a half an hour to kickoff and all you crave is meat and potatoes. Forget the grill. Forget the plates. You can even forget the knife and fork. You're just a step away from being the gameday gourmet.

Creamy Bean Dip

Beans, beans, the magical fruit. The more you make, the more they'll hoot.

What you'll need:

1 pound ground beef
Salt, to taste
Freshly ground black
   pepper, to taste
Olive oil
1 large onion, minced
2 cans refried beans
1 16-ounce jar of your
   favorite salsa

1 8-ounce package cream
   cheese
3 tablespoons sour cream
Sliced jalapeño peppers,
   to taste
1/2 cup shredded
   Cheddar cheese
Tortilla chips

What to do:

Season the beef with salt and pepper to your liking. Heat the olive oil in a skillet and sauté the beef and onion.

Combine the beans, salsa, cream cheese, sour cream, and the jalapeños in a large mixing bowl while the meat is cooking. Mix well. Drain the beef and onions and add them to the bean mixture. Add the cheese and mix thoroughly. Let the dip stand for 30 minutes. Serve warm with your favorite tortilla chips.

Yield: 6 to 8 servings

41

TAILGATING

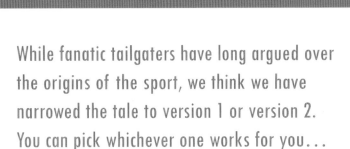

While fanatic tailgaters have long argued over the origins of the sport, we think we have narrowed the tale to version 1 or version 2. You can pick whichever one works for you...

The Tailgating Tale, Version 1:

Tailgating dates back to the very first college football game between Rutgers and Princeton in 1869, when fans traveled to the game by carriage, grilling sausages and burgers at the "tail end" of the horse. Today tailgating is a part of most athletic events, especially college football.

The Tailgating Tale, Version 2:

It all began at Yale in 1904. (At least that's what they'll tell you.) Is it true? While other schools have claimed the honor, the Yale story has been verified by, you guessed it ...Yale. This is how the Yale story goes: Once upon a time, there was a train made up of private railcars that brought fans to a Yale game. The train stopped at the station, and the fans had to walk the distance to the stadium. When they arrived at the stadium, they were hungry and thirsty. So, the next time they went to a game, they brought along a picnic basket of food for the next game. Thus, the concept of tailgating was born.

The 5 Tailgating Commandments

1) Make a list of the things to bring: frozen bottles of water (for the cooler), condiments, extra ice, comfortable shoes, jumper cables, toilet paper, rain gear, sun block, first-aid kit, plastic trash bags, antacid, napkins, paper towels, forks, spoons, damp towels in a zippered bag, and maybe a friend or two.

2) Plan your menu ahead, and do the shopping and prep work a day or two before the game. Keep it simple!

3) Plan to arrive 3 to 4 hours early and to stay 1 to 2 hours after the game. Tailgating is an all-day event.

4) Meet your fellow tailgaters! Throw a football with friends, listen to a few games, take some pictures, dress in your team colors, paint your face (Really, guys, stick to the face, okay?). In other words, it's a party, so act like it and have some fun!

5) Schedule the main meal for about an hour and a half before the game starts. Give yourself plenty of time to eat, clean up, and thoroughly extinguish those tailgating fires and cool off those hot hibachis before hitting the bleachers for the game.

Mini Meatloaves

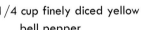

What you'll need:

1 pound ground beef
1 pound ground sausage
2 eggs
1/2 cup Italian seasoned
   breadcrumbs
1 tablespoon minced garlic
1/2 cup minced onion
1/4 cup finely diced green
   bell pepper

1/4 cup finely diced yellow
   bell pepper
1/4 cup finely diced orange
   bell pepper
2 tablespoons
   Worcestershire sauce
Standard-sized muffin pan

What to do:

Preheat the oven to 400°F. Combine the meat, eggs, breadcrumbs, garlic, onion, peppers, and Worcestershire sauce in a large mixing bowl. Mix the ingredients by hand for about five minutes, or until the mixture is blended evenly. Pack the mixture into the muffin cups until they are even with the top of the tin. Place the filled muffin pan on a baking sheet to catch the drippings. Reduce the oven heat to 375°F and bake the meatloaves for 30 minutes, or until the tops are browned and the juice runs clear.

Mini-Meatloaf Mini-tip: Add a little zip by topping the loaves with a thin layer of ketchup, mushroom gravy, or barbecue sauce prior to baking.

Yield: about 8 to 12 minis

Get your meatloaf fix in bite-size form. Just because they're smaller doesn't mean they're less impressive.

Partychoke & Cheese Dip

Don't be intimidated by artichokes. They may look tough and pointy on the outside, but they have hearts, like you and me—and they're delicious! Impress partygoers with this heart-y party dip.

What you'll need:

2 14-ounce cans of artichoke hearts, drained
1 cup freshly grated Parmesan cheese
1 tablespoon minced lemon zest
1 tablespoon freshly ground black pepper
Hot pepper sauce, to taste
8 ounces light cream cheese
1/2 cup bread crumbs
1 cup amber ale
Oil or shortening, for greasing the baking dish
Chips or crackers

What to do:

Combine the artichoke hearts, Parmesan cheese, lemon zest, pepper, hot pepper sauce, cream cheese, bread crumbs, and ale in a large mixing bowl. Mix well. Pour the mixture into a serving dish and serve with your favorite chips or crackers.

Optional: For warm dip, add 1 egg white to the mixture. Preheat the oven to 350°F and bake for 30 minutes.

Yield: 6 to 8 servings

Spicy Beer-Battered Onion Rings

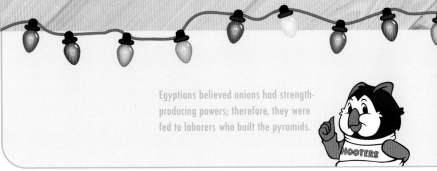

Egyptians believed onions had strength-producing powers; therefore, they were fed to laborers who built the pyramids.

What you'll need:

- 1 cup all-purpose flour, plus extra for dusting
- 1 cup of your favorite beer
- 2 tablespoons of your favorite hot sauce
- 1 tablespoon freshly ground black pepper
- 2 Vidalia onions, peeled, cut crosswise, and separated into 1/3-inch thick rings
- Vegetable oil, for frying
- Salt, to taste
- Paper towels

What to do:

Put the flour into a bowl and make a "well" in the center with a spoon. Pour the beer, hot sauce, and black pepper into the "well" and whisk until the mixture is just combined. Strain the batter into a clean bowl and allow it to rest, covered, for 1 hour.

Preheat 2 inches of oil to about 370°F. Dust the onion rings with the additional flour, shaking off the excess, then dip and coat them with the batter. Fry batches of onion rings in the heated oil until they are golden. Transfer fried onions with a slotted spoon to paper towels to remove excess oil. Salt to taste.

Yield: 6 to 8 servings

Batter up! Your taste buds will do "the wave" when these crunchy rings slide into home.

BEER

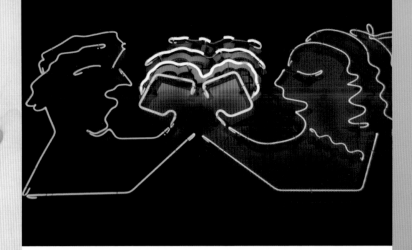

Useless Beer Facts:

You would think that because of its name, Munich's annual 16-day Oktoberfest is in October, but it actually begins in mid-September and ends on the first Sunday in October.

In their efforts to regulate beer quality, the ancient Babylonians, who were among history's earliest brewers, decreed that any commercial beermaker who sold unfit beer would be drowned in his/her own libations— a fitting end to a very serious crime.

According to a diary entry from a passenger on the *Mayflower*, the pilgrims landed at Plymouth Rock, rather than continue to their destination in Virginia, due to lack of beer. Serious crises were averted.

In English pubs, as we all know, ale is ordered by pints and quarts. So in Jolly Olde England, when customers got unruly, the bartender would yell at them to mind their own pints and quarts and settle down. That's where we get the phrase "mind your P's and Q's."

After consuming a bucket or two of vibrant brew called aul, or ale, the Vikings would head fearlessly into battle, often without armor or even shirts. In Norse, the word for "no shirt" is "berserk," which their wild battles came to be known as.

Beer-ish Quotes

"The problem with the world is that everyone is a few drinks behind."
—Humphrey Bogart

"Always remember that I have taken more out of alcohol than alcohol has taken out of me."
—Winston Churchill

"Beer is proof that God loves us and wants us to be happy."
—Benjamin Franklin

"I am a firm believer in the people. If given the truth, they can be depended upon to meet any national crisis. The great point is to bring them the real facts, and beer."
—Abraham Lincoln

"May your glass be ever full. May the roof over your head be always strong. And may you be in heaven half an hour before the devil knows you're dead."
—Old Irish Toast

Know your BEERS

Lager

A type of beer of German origin that contains a relatively small amount of hops and is aged from six weeks to six months to allow sedimentation. Golden, sparkling and crisp, Lagers are best enjoyed at cooler-than-room temperature.

Bock Beer

Heavier than lager and darkened by high-coloured malts, bock is traditionally brewed in the winter for drinking during the spring.

Ale

Fruity and bitter, ale is similar to but heavier than beer and contains more hops. It is best enjoyed at room temperature or slightly warmer.

Porter and Stout

Stouts and porters are characterized by darkness and depth. Both types of beer are delicious with hearty meat stews and surprisingly good with shellfish.

Dry

"Dry" refers to the amount of residual sugar left in a beer following fermentation. This type of beer is fermented longer than normal brews so that practically all of the residual sugar is converted into alcohol. The result is a beer that has a crisp flavor, clean finish and very little aftertaste.

Brown Sugar-Baked Beans

Brown sugar... How come you taste
so good (with beans)?

The odds that the beans in your side dish of baked beans came from North Dakota, Michigan or Nebraska are 50-50. 60 percent of the nation's dry, edible beans come from those three states.

What you'll need:

4 slices bacon
1/2 cup firmly packed brown sugar
1/2 cup chopped onion
2 16-ounce cans pork and beans
2 tablespoons Dijon mustard
1 tablespoon Worcestershire sauce
1/4 teaspoon hot pepper sauce
Paper towels

What to do:

Preheat the oven to 325°F. Cook the bacon over medium-high heat in a skillet, turning occasionally until browned. Remove excess grease from the bacon strips by patting them with paper towels. Crumble the bacon into bite-size pieces.

Combine the cooked bacon, brown sugar, onion, beans, mustard, Worcestershire sauce, and hot pepper sauce into an ungreased casserole dish. Bake, stirring occasionally, for about 1 1/2 hours, or until the beans have thickened slightly.

Yield: 4 servings

Mama Sue's Chili

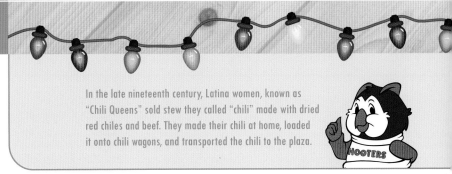

In the late nineteenth century, Latina women, known as "Chili Queens" sold stew they called "chili" made with dried red chiles and beef. They made their chili at home, loaded it onto chili wagons, and transported the chili to the plaza.

What you'll need:

- 1 1/2 pounds ground beef or ground turkey
- 1 large Vidalia onion, chopped
- 4 16-ounce cans New Orleans-style kidney beans
- 1 (10 ¾-ounce) can tomato soup
- 1 16-ounce can tomato sauce
- 2 packages McCormick's Chili Seasoning Mix
- Shredded cheese (Cheddar or Jack), for garnish
- Sour cream, for garnish
- Oyster crackers (optional)

What to do:

Brown the beef and chopped onion together in a large skillet. Place the cooked meat and onions in a large stew pot over medium-high heat. Add in the kidney beans, tomato soup, tomato sauce, and chili seasoning. Heat until the mixture starts to bubble, stirring every 2 minutes. Reduce the heat and let the chili simmer for 30 minutes, stirring every 5 minutes.

Serve in a bowl with shredded cheese and sour cream on top. Complement with oyster crackers, if desired.

Yield: 6 to 8 servings

Tip for the chili connoisseur:

For even better chili, refrigerate the leftovers and reheat. This chili is better the next day after all the flavors have blended.

Mike McNeil, VP of marketing at HOA says this about his mom's chili: "I grew up eating this chili. My mother, Sue McNeil, is a practical and resourceful lady who takes common ingredients and turns them into culinary masterpieces. This was always a favorite when the weather was cold."

54

Sinfully Delicious Bread Bowl

When your buddies ask how you came up with this recipe, just tell them the Devil made you do it.

The Latin proverb *Sine Cerere et Libero, friget Venus* translates as "Without bread and wine, love is cold."

What you'll need:

- 1 16-ounce round loaf country white bread
- 8 ounces softened cream cheese
- 8 ounces sour cream
- 1 teaspoon Dale's Sauce
- 2 green onions, finely chopped
- 2 ounces Virginia baked ham, finely chopped
- 2 cups shredded sharp Cheddar cheese

What to do:

Preheat the oven to 350°F. Hollow out the bread loaf to create a bread bowl. Cut the extracted bread dough into cubes and place the cubes on a cookie sheet. Combine the cream cheese, sour cream, Dale's Sauce, onions, ham, and Cheddar in a large bowl. Transfer the mixture into the bread bowl and place the bowl on the cookie sheet with the bread cubes. Bake in the oven for 20 minutes, remove the bread cubes, then bake the bread bowl for 10 more minutes. Serve with skewers or long forks for dipping the bread pieces into the bowl.

Yield: 6 to 8 servings

Tip for the Yankee boy:

Dale's Sauce is a soy-based seasoning sauce found primarily in the South or online.

Chip's Grits Galore

What you'll need:

- 4 cups water
- 1 1/3 cups milk
- 1 1/2 cups quick-cooking grits
- 4 ounces cream cheese
- 1 cup shredded Cheddar cheese
- 8 slices bacon, crisp-cooked and crumbled
- 1 10-ounce can tomatoes with green chiles
- Additional crumbled bacon for garnish

What to do:

Combine the water and milk in a 2-quart saucepan. Bring to a boil and stir in the grits. Return to a boil, reduce heat, and cover. Simmer 5 to 7 minutes, adding more water if needed.

Add the cream cheese and the Cheddar to the grits. Cook until the cheeses melt, stirring constantly. Stir in the bacon and tomatoes with chiles. Spoon into a serving bowl, garnish with crumbled bacon, and serve.

Yield: 4 to 6 servings

The annual World Grits Festival is held in April at St. George, South Carolina.

The town claims to be the "Grits Capital of the World," eating more pounds of grits per capita than anyplace else in the world.

In 2002 Georgia designated grits as the official state prepared food.

TAILGATING

& GRILLING

The history of grilling begins 500,000 years ago, at about the time early man cracked two rocks together and burned himself with the new invention of fire. In the 1940s, grilling moved from campsites and picnics into the backyard, thanks to the baby boom and the post World War II migration to the suburbs. By the 1950s, a man wasn't a man unless he had a shiny new sedan in the driveway, 2.5 kids, a dog, and a grill in the backyard.

Fire-in-the-Hole Kabobs

Pull the pin and grit your teeth, soldier, 'cause these kabobs will blow you away!

What you'll need:

1 1/2 pounds sirloin steak, cut into 1/2-inch cubes
3 beef bouillon cubes
1 tablespoon water
3 teaspoons cayenne pepper
1 teaspoon freshly ground black pepper
1/2 teaspoon salt
2 tablespoons vegetable oil
Wooden skewers

 Plan Ahead Alert! The meat will need to marinate overnight. Also, soak the wooden skewers in water overnight to prevent the meat from sticking.

What to do:

Crumble the bouillon cubes into the water in a large mixing bowl, and stir to create a thick paste. Stir in the cayenne pepper, black pepper, and salt. Add the meat and swirl thoroughly to coat. Skewer the meat with the wooden skewers. Place the skewers in a covered container and refrigerate overnight.

Fire up the grill. Brush oil onto both the kabobs and the grill. Place the kabobs on the grill and cook on each side for 2 to 3 minutes.

Yield: 3 servings

Chic-kabobs

Eating food on a stick prevents unnecessary hand-washing, which saves water. Do your part for the environment by eating all your food on a stick. We recommend starting with this easy-to-make, tasty recipe.

What you'll need:

1 1/2 cups prepared teriyaki marinade
1/2 cup water
1/4 cup olive oil
1/4 cup minced garlic
1/4 cup toasted sesame seeds

6 chicken breasts, thawed and cut into 1-inch cubes
1 onion, cut into 1-inch cubes
1 green pepper, cut into 1-inch squares
24 white mushrooms
Wooden skewers

 Plan Ahead Alert! Soak the wooden skewers in water overnight to prevent the meat from sticking.

What to do:

Combine the teriyaki marinade, water, olive oil, garlic, and sesame seeds in a mixing bowl. Throw the cubed chicken breasts, onion, green pepper, mushrooms, and sauce into a large, zippered freezer bag, then zip it shut, and shake vigorously. Put the freezer bag of goodies in the fridge (or in a cooler if you're tailgating) for at least an hour.

Shake the freezer bag vigorously again about a half-hour before grilling, then fire up the grill. Skewer the chicken once the coals are hot. Place about 3 pieces of chicken per skewer with a mix of the veggies between each one. Grill the kabobs for 10 to 15 minutes, or until the chicken is no longer pink, brushing occasionally with leftover marinade and turning every 5 minutes.

Yield: 4 to 6 servings

Grilled Chicken Satay

Some say that satay was actually invented by Chinese immigrants in India who sold the skewered barbecue meat on the street.

What's a satay, you say? Just a kabob made the Indonesian way. Treat your taste buds to an exotic vacation.

 Plan Ahead Alert! Chicken needs to chill for at least 4 hours before cooking. Also, soak the wooden skewers in water overnight to keep the meat from sticking.

What to do:

Preparing the Chicken Satay:
Cut the chicken into strips, 4 inches long by 1/2 inch wide. Set aside. Stir the coconut milk, fish sauce, brown sugar, cilantro, and curry powder together in a large mixing bowl. Add the chicken and stir until evenly coated. Cover the meat and refrigerate for at least 4 hours.

Fire up the grill. Remove the chicken from the marinade. Skewer two pieces of chicken onto each skewer. Brush the hot grill with the olive oil before placing the skewers onto the grill to prevent the chicken from sticking. Grill until the chicken is golden brown, about 10 minutes total, turning occasionally. Place the chicken on a serving plate, and serve with a bowl of peanut sauce.

Preparing the Peanut Sauce:
Purée the peanut butter, garlic, soy sauce, sugar, water, salt, and pepper in a blender until the mixture is smooth. Transfer the sauce to a serving bowl and serve with the chicken.

Yield: 6 to 8 servings

What you'll need:

For the Chicken Satay:
1 1/2 pounds boneless, skinless chicken thighs
1/2 cup coconut milk
1/4 cup fish sauce
3 tablespoons brown sugar
2 tablespoons chopped fresh cilantro
1 tablespoon curry powder
1 tablespoon olive oil
4 ounces peanut sauce (see recipe to the right)
Wooden skewers

For the Peanut Sauce:
1/3 cup creamy peanut butter
1 clove garlic
2 tablespoons soy sauce
1 teaspoon sugar
1/3 cup water
Salt, to taste
Freshly ground black pepper, to taste

Shrimp on a Stick

Oddly enough, shrimp can only swim backwards, and their hearts are in their heads.

What you'll need:

2 dozen large, fresh shrimp, peeled and deveined
1 stick butter, melted
Prepared barbecue sauce, for brushing
1 jar cocktail sauce, if desired
Wooden skewers

 Plan Ahead Alert! Soak the wooden skewers in water overnight to prevent the meat from sticking.

What to do:

Skewer six shrimp onto each skewer and refrigerate them until you are ready to grill. Fire up the grill. Place the skewered shrimp on the grill and brush first with the melted butter then with barbeque sauce. Grill for 2 minutes, flip, and brush with the butter and barbecue sauce. Grill for 2 more minutes. Serve with cocktail sauce, if desired.

Yield: 4 shrimp sticks

Did you know that Americans consume an average of 1 billion pounds of shrimp every year? Do your patriotic duty by making this recipe and sharing it with all your buddies.

Roasted Veggie Mishmash

What you'll need:

For the tomato vinaigrette:
4 sun-dried tomatoes, chopped
1/4 cup red wine vinegar
9 cloves garlic, chopped
1/4 teaspoon dried red pepper flakes
1/2 cup olive oil

For the veggies:
2 large portobello mushrooms, washed, stemmed, and julienned

1 yellow summer squash, diced
1 red pepper, cut into 1-inch cubes
1 eggplant, cut crosswise into 1-inch cubes
1/4 cup olive oil, for brushing
Salt, to taste
Freshly ground black pepper, to taste
Foil roasting bag or aluminum foil

What to do:

Preparing the tomato vinaigrette:
Place the sun-dried tomatoes, wine vinegar, garlic, and red pepper flakes in a blender and blend until smooth. Slowly add the 1/2-cup portion of olive oil until emulsified (that means really mixed up).

Grilling the veggies:
Fire up the grill. Place the cut veggies and mushrooms into a bowl, brush them with the 1/4-cup portion of olive oil and season with salt and pepper. Place the veggies and mushrooms in a foil roasting bag or aluminum foil. Grill for approximately 10 to 12 minutes, or to desired doneness. Arrange on a platter and top with the tomato vinaigrette.

Yield: 4 to 6 servings

Skewers O' Fish

A favorite of salty fishermen coast to coast, this could be the fish dish you like the most.

What you'll need:

1 pound firm white fish, filleted and skinned
1 teaspoon sea salt
1/2 cup plain yogurt
2 tablespoons Tabasco sauce
2 tablespoons honey
1 tablespoon coriander
1 tablespoon cayenne pepper
1 lemon, cut into wedges
Wooden skewers

 Plan Ahead Alert! The fish will need to marinate in the fridge for at least 2 hours. Soak the wooden skewers in water overnight to prevent the meat from sticking.

What to do:

Cut the fish into 1 1/2-inch cubes. Skewer about five pieces of fish onto each skewer. Sprinkle with sea salt. Combine the yogurt, Tabasco, honey, coriander, and cayenne pepper in a small mixing bowl, and mix to make a paste. Spread the yogurt paste directly onto the fish and place in the refrigerator for about 2 to 3 hours.

Fire up the grill. Place the skewers on the grill for about 10 minutes, or until the fish can be easily flaked with a fork. Garnish with lemon wedges and serve.

Yield: 3 servings

GRILLING

For a taste that'll make the ol' lady blush, get rid of that ol' basting brush!

Basting brushes are great for beginners, but they'll wear your wings out by forcing you to dip back in the sauce more than a pro like you needs to. Plus, basting brushes are too weak to handle bulky spices, causing them to fall back into the bowl on their trip to the steak. For getting the most out of fine sauces, oils, beer, and wine, use a mister or spray bottle. And for thick and chunky marinades, use a professional "meat mop" (yes, they look exactly like what they sound like).

Grill away unwanted fat by keeping the flame away from that.

For cooking the fat out of steaks and roasts, you might be thinking, "Put the flame to 'er!" But doing so can char your meats—Yuck!—and cause flare-ups that will inspire the family to demote you from Grill-Meister to Dish-Meister in no time. You can keep 911 off speed-dial and keep everyone's eyebrows intact if you arrange the coals in a ring beneath the meat and place a drip pan in the middle to catch high-octane grease fuels. Plus, with the flame out of contact with the meat, you can cook at higher temperatures, yielding a crispier outside and a juicier inside.

Keep your food tasting go-oood!——Throw away the lighter fluid!

Though inexpensive and really fast, lighter fluid tastes like gas. That's great if you're a gas-guzzling stock car, but for flavor-loving meat eaters, we recommend replacing bio-fuels with non-toxic paraffin cubes or wood chips. For a truly "organic" experience, get back to basics with a charcoal or wood-coal cooker.

P.S.

Don't add BBQ sauce until food is almost done, as it could cause the food to burn.

Turn meat once during cooking using tongs or a spatula; do not use a fork, it could pierce the meat and allow the juices to run out.

Marinate in a food-safe plastic bag or non-reactive container such as glass or ceramic, not aluminum.

GAS vs. CHARCOAL

Taste or convenience?

The charcoal, vs. gas issue is largely a taste vs convenience issue. Oddly enough, taste tests actually reveal no significant flavor difference between gas and charcoal grills. And what's not to like about gas grills. They're ready when you are. They're easy to clean, and there are no ashes to dump or coals to deal with. Bottom line: The majority of barbecue grill owners have gas grills and love them.

Every barbecue cook-off contestant, however, swears by the charcoal. Using anything else would be offensive. Charcoal grills are simpler and less expensive, and they're gaining in features and convenience, too.

But if it's not a matter of superior taste (and we're not choosing sides), why *would* anyone fool with charcoal? Admit it, you love being Master and Commander of the Coals. It's not an easy job, but it sure is satisfying.

Environmental concerns

Charcoal grills are worse environmentally because of their smoke and noxious lighter fluid fumes. But you can eliminate fumes by using a charcoal chimney starter to light your coals. They're simple and cheap.

Gas grills are somewhere in between. They use propane or natural gas, which are at least natural products and only mildly noxious.

Thai Chili Shrimp

What you'll need:

- 12 ounces porter
- 1/3 cup toasted sesame oil
- 1 tablespoon frozen lime juice concentrate
- 2 tablespoons Thai fish sauce
- 5 cloves garlic, peeled and crushed
- 2 tablespoons grated fresh ginger
- 1 teaspoon powdered cardamom
- 1 teaspoon Thai red chili paste
- 1 1/2 pounds medium shrimp, heads removed, shells on
- 10 bamboo skewers

 Plan Ahead Alert! The shrimp need to marinate in the fridge overnight. Also, soak the bamboo skewers in water overnight to prevent the meat from sticking.

What to do:

Create a marinade by whisking together the porter, sesame oil, lime juice, fish sauce, garlic, ginger, cardamom, and chili paste in a mixing bowl.

Rinse the shrimp and place them in a large, zippered freezer bag. Pour in the marinade, zip the bag closed, and refrigerate overnight.

Fire up the grill. Spear three shrimp onto each bamboo skewer. Grill the shrimp for about 40 to 60 seconds on each side, or until the shells turn an orange-pink color.

Yield: 3 servings

Flamingos turn pink from eating shrimp because of their beta-carotene content. Flamingos that don't eat shrimp are white and not pink. If we humans ate nothing but carrots (which also contain beta-carotene), our skin would have an orangish tint to it.

This dish isn't as refined as Dungeness crab or as tacky as hot dogs, but your guests will be satisfied and maybe even a little impressed. Why not bring a little slice of Bangkok to your table?

Tin Man Special

Aluminum foil is the most common "utensil" used in the preparation of side dishes for the grill.

The most popular barbecue utensils are long-handled tongs (81%), followed by grill cleaning brushes (75%), and then long-handled forks and spatulas (tied at 64%).

Cod. Wrap it up. Grill it up. Serve it up. Cod.

What you'll need:

1 pound cod
3 tablespoons unsalted butter
1/4 cup freshly squeezed lemon juice
1 teaspoon dry thyme
1 teaspoon dry dill weed
1 teaspoon sea salt
1/4 teaspoon freshly ground black pepper
1 teaspoon paprika
1 onion, thinly sliced
Aluminum foil

What to do:

Fire up the grill.

Cut two 12 by 12-inch squares of aluminum foil, and set aside. Season 1 tablespoon of the butter with the lemon juice, thyme, dill weed, sea salt, and pepper in a small saucepan. Heat over low heat on the stove until the butter is melted. Lay each piece of cod on a sheet of aluminum foil. Pour equal amounts of the seasoned butter over each portion of cod.

Sprinkle each piece of fish with paprika, and top with the sliced onions. Wrap the foil securely around the fish. Grill for 4 to 6 minutes on each side.

Yield: 2 servings

Caballero Steak

What you'll need:

- 1 pound beef round steak
- 1/3 cup vegetable oil
- 1/3 cup freshly squeezed lime juice
- 2 jalapeño peppers, seeded and chopped
- 2 shallots, chopped
- 2 tablespoons chopped fresh cilantro
- 2 cloves fresh garlic, chopped
- Salt, to taste
- 1/2 teaspoon freshly ground black pepper
- 1 tablespoon paprika

 Plan Ahead Alert! Steak needs to marinate for at least 6 hours, or overnight, before cooking.

What to do:

Stir together the oil, lime juice, jalapeño peppers, shallots, cilantro, garlic, salt, pepper, and paprika in a small mixing bowl. Place the steak in a large, zippered freezer bag, and set the bag upright in a shallow dish. Pour the marinade over the steak and seal the bag. Marinate in the refrigerator for about 6 hours, or overnight, turning the bag occasionally.

Fire up the grill. Drain the steak, reserving the marinade in a small mixing bowl. Grill the steak on an open grill to desired doneness. Brush occasionally with marinade up until the last 5 minutes of grilling.

Yield: 2 servings

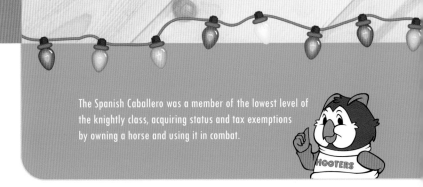

The Spanish Caballero was a member of the lowest level of the knightly class, acquiring status and tax exemptions by owning a horse and using it in combat.

After a long day in the saddle, all you want is a cold beer and big ol' piece of meat. This steak is so hot, it'll kick you in the teeth.

Scotty's Swordfish with Sweet Corn Relish

Swordfish are the fastest swimming fish in the world. They're delicious (if you can catch one).

This is one dish guaranteed to hook your taste buds and reel your hunger into shore.

What you'll need:

12 ounces swordfish

For the marinade:
2 tablespoons chopped
   fresh cilantro
2 tablespoons olive oil
1 fresh garlic clove,
   crushed
1/2 teaspoon freshly
   ground black pepper

For the relish:
1 cup fresh or unfrozen
   corn kernels
1/2 cup diced tomato
1 jalapeño pepper, seeded
   and chopped
2 tablespoons rice vinegar
1 tablespoon unsalted
   butter
1/2 teaspoon kosher salt
1/2 teaspoon freshly
   ground black pepper

Plan Ahead Alert! Swordfish will need to marinate for at least 2 hours before cooking.

What to do:

Preparing the marinade:
Combine the cilantro, oil, garlic, and pepper in a small bowl and mix well. Coat the fish evenly with mixture. Cover and marinate in the refrigerator for at least 2 hours.

Preparing the relish:
Combine the corn, tomato, jalapeño, vinegar, butter, salt, and pepper in a small saucepan. Place the pan over medium-high heat on the stove until the butter is melted. Remove the pan from the heat and mix well. Cover and keep the pan warm while grilling the fish.

Grilling the swordfish:
Fire up the grill. Brush the grill with oil. Grill the swordfish for about 4 minutes per side, or until the fish can be easily flaked with a fork. Remove the fish from the grill and place it onto a serving plate. Garnish with the warm corn relish.

Yield: 4 servings

Did you know?

Sleeping bags reflect body heat back to you, and you can reflect the most body heat by sleeping in your birthday suit!

If you are camping in bear country, be sure to cook your meals at least 300 feet downwind of your sleeping area. Doing so will lead those hungry bears astray and keep them from bear-all-ing in on your party.

Use baking soda to eliminate cooking odors in your clothing, and, remember the part about the birthday suit when you return to your tent for the night.

Foil the Soot!

You know that ugly black soot that gets all over the bottom of your pots and pans when you cook over an open fire? You can avoid the messy cleanup if you use one of those aluminum foil pans or pie tins under your cooking pot. The foil transmits heat and collects most of that stubborn soot.

Friendly Fishing Tips:

- The best day of the year to go fishing is the first day of school.

- Be gentle, and release undersized trout as soon as possible—it's very traumatic for the slippery little guys.

- When you release a completely exhausted fish, hold it upright in the water long enough for it to regain its strength before letting it battle a strong current.

- When gathering night crawlers after dark, use a flashlight with red cellophane over the lens. A white light may scare them back into their holes.

- Just after heavy rains, crawlers often cover sidewalks and roads. But, picking up a slippery night crawler can be frustrating and time consuming. Instead, try using a spatula.

CAUTION BEAR XING

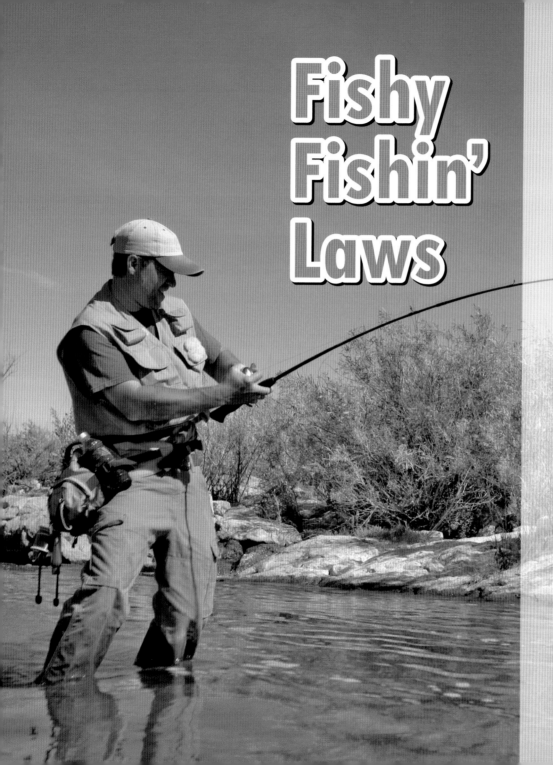

Fishy Fishin' Laws

Delaware: It is against the law for a newlywed husband to go fishing during his honeymoon.

Nebraska: It is illegal to go whale fishing.

Oklahoma: Fish may not be contained in fishbowls while on a public bus. Whaling is illegal.

Washington: In Seattle, it is illegal to carry a fishbowl or aquarium onto a bus because the sound of the water sloshing may disturb other passengers.

Wyoming: Using a firearm to fish is strictly forbidden.

Georgia: In Ackworth, all households must own fishing poles.

Idaho: You may not fish on a camel's back. Residents may not fish from a giraffe's back.

Illinois: It is forbidden to fish while sitting on a giraffe's neck. A law in Oblong makes it a crime to make love while fishing or hunting on your wedding day.

Indiana: No one may catch a fish with his bare hands.

Kansas: No one may catch fish with his bare hands.

Kentucky: It's illegal to fish in the Ohio River in Kentucky without an Indiana fishing license. It is also illegal to fish anywhere in the state with a bow and arrow.

Montana: It is illegal for married women to go fishing alone on Sundays, and illegal for an unmarried woman to fish alone at all.

New Jersey: It is against the law for a man to knit during the fishing season.

Ohio: It is illegal to get a fish drunk. It is illegal to fish for whales on Sunday.

Oregon: Canned corn is not to be used as bait for fishing.

Pennsylvania: You may not catch a fish with any body part except the mouth. You may not catch a fish with your hands. Dynamite is not to be used to catch fish.

Tennessee: It is illegal to use a lasso to catch a fish. You can't shoot any game other than whales from a moving automobile.

Utah: It is against the law to fish from horseback. It is considered an offense to hunt whales.

Grilled Steak with Mango Salsa

Freshen up the dog days of summer; add a little mango and lime to make an ordinary steak sublime.

What you'll need:

3 8-ounce round steaks
Salt, to taste
Freshly ground black pepper, to taste

For the marinade:
1/4 cup freshly squeezed lime juice
2 tablespoons minced green onion
2 tablespoons water
2 teaspoons minced fresh ginger
2 tablespoons minced fresh garlic
1/4 teaspoon salt

For the mango salsa:
1 1/2 cups finely chopped fresh mango
2 tablespoons minced green onion
1 tablespoon freshly squeezed lime juice
1 tablespoon minced fresh cilantro
1 jalapeño pepper, seeded and finely chopped

 Plan Ahead Alert! The steak needs to marinate in the fridge for at least 6 hours, or overnight, before grilling.

What to do:

Preparing the marinade:
Combine the lime juice, green onion, water, ginger, garlic, and salt into a large mixing bowl. Mix well. Place the steaks and marinade in a large, zippered freezer bag. Zip up the bag and shake to mix well. Place the bag in a large bowl in the fridge for at least 6 hours, or overnight, turning occasionally.

Preparing the salsa:
Combine the mango, green onion, lime juice, cilantro, and the jalapeño into a medium bowl and toss together.

Grilling the steak:
Fire up the grill. Remove the steak from the marinade and place it on the grill. Grill, covered, for about 10 minutes per side, or to desired doneness. Carve steak into thin slices, and salt and pepper to taste. Serve with mango salsa.

Yield: 3 servings

Drunken Chicken

Grilled Garden Herb Kabobs

Grilling is more fun when your meat is drunker than you are. In the backyard or in a parking lot, this recipe is sure to make the crowd go wild.

What you'll need:

1 whole chicken, defrosted
Your favorite grilling spices
1 can of beer
Paper towels

Warning! Be sure to open the beer can before grilling to avoid turning your grill into an unwanted chicken-and-beer bomb.

What to do:

Fire up the grill. Rinse the chicken thoroughly with cold water (no soap) while the coals are heating up. Pat dry with paper towels. Rub the outside of the chicken with your favorite spices. Open a can of beer, and set it upright in the center of the grill once the coals are ready. Place the spiced-up chicken onto the opened can so it appears that the chicken is sitting on it. Cover the grill and relax, knowing that while it's cooking the chicken will be getting sauced. Grill until the meat begins to fall off the bone.

Yield: 1 to 4 servings, depending on appetites and the size of the chicken

What you'll need:

For the kabobs
2 ears corn, husked and cut into thirds
3 medium zucchinis, cut into quarters
1 large onion, peeled and cut into 12 wedges
6 cherry tomatoes
12 large mushrooms, cleaned and stemmed
2 green bell peppers, cut into 2-inch squares
6 12-inch metal skewers

For the herb spread:
1/2 cup salted butter, melted
1 teaspoon chopped fresh chives
1 teaspoon chopped fresh oregano
Salt, to taste
Freshly ground black pepper, to taste

What to do:

Fire up the grill.

Boil the corn in a 2-quart saucepan on the stove for a few minutes. Place the cut veggies on the skewers, alternating the corn, zucchini, onion, tomatoes, mushrooms, and peppers, reserving a 4-inch space at the end of each skewer.

Combine the butter, chives, oregano, salt, and pepper in a small bowl and mix well. Grill the kabobs, turning occasionally, for about 10 minutes. Brush the herb spread onto the kabobs, and continue grilling and turning until the vegetables are crisp but tender, about 8 to 12 more minutes.

Yield: 4 servings

Grilled Mini Poppers

What you'll need:

- 1/2 cup sour cream
- 20 sweet mini peppers
- 8 ounces softened cream cheese
- 1 tomato (4 ounces), cored, seeded, and chopped
- 1/3 cup chopped red onion
- 1/3 cup chopped fresh cilantro
- 3/4 teaspoon kosher salt
- Paprika, to dust

What to do:

Spoon the sour cream into a large, zippered freezer bag. Chill.

Fire up the grill.

Rinse the peppers and cut them in half lengthwise through the stems. Scoop out and discard the seeds and veins. Mix the cream cheese, tomato, onion, cilantro, and salt in a medium-sized bowl. Spoon the mixture evenly into the pepper halves, pressing it into the hollows with your thumb or with the back of a spoon, and sprinkle with paprika.

Place the filled peppers on the grill, cheese-side up. Grill over medium heat, until the peppers are blistered and slightly charred on the bottoms, about 3 to 5 minutes. Transfer the peppers to a plate. Squeeze dollops of sour cream equally over the hot peppers and serve.

Yield: 8 to 10 servings

Philadelphia® brand cream cheese is one of the oldest American packaged foods; it went on sale in its protective wrapper in 1885.

Looking to add some flare to the evening meal? These poppers are dy-no-mite!

Coby's Samurai Rib-Eye

After a hard day in battle, even the fiercest warrior must set down his *katana* and recover with a good meal.

What you'll need:

3 rib-eye steaks
3/4 cup prepared teriyaki sauce
2 tablespoons dry sherry
1 tablespoon chopped fresh ginger

 Plan Ahead Alert! The steaks need to marinate in the fridge for at least 6 hours, or overnight, before grilling.

What to do:

Combine the teriyaki sauce, sherry, and ginger in a small bowl and mix well. Place the steaks and marinade in a large, zippered freezer bag. Zip up the bag, and shake to mix well. Place the bag in a large bowl in the fridge for at least 6 hours, or overnight, turning occasionally.

Fire up the grill. Remove the steaks from the plastic bag and place them on the grill. (If you are using briquettes, they should be medium, ash-covered coals.) Cover and grill to desired doneness, turning occasionally.

Yield: 3 servings

Grilled Portobello Mushrooms

These mushrooms may not alter your vision, but they'll sure make your taste buds hallucinate...

What you'll need:

4 large portobello mushrooms, washed and stemmed
1/4 cup extra virgin olive oil
1 tablespoon chopped fresh garlic
1 tablespoon chopped green onion
Freshly ground black pepper, to taste

What to do:

Fire up the grill.

Mix the oil, garlic, onions, and pepper together in a small bowl. Brush the mushrooms thoroughly with half of the seasoned oil mixture. Grill with the caps away from the heat for 5 minutes, or until they begin to brown. Brush with the remaining oil, and turn. Grill for an additional 5 minutes and serve.

Yield: 4 servings

RECIPES to

IMPRESS

How to Impress a Woman: Compliment her, snuggle her, kiss her, caress her, love her, tease her, comfort her, protect her, hug her, hold her, spend money on her, wine & dine her, buy things for her, listen to her, care for her, stand by her, support her, tell that she's beautiful, send her for a girls' weekend at the beach, give her your credit cards, go to the ends of the earth for her....

How to Impress a Man: Show up and bring beer.

Coconut Shrimp

When your guests complain about the endless bowls of guacamole and stale chips, bowl them over with a tropical tsunami of flavor.

 Plan Ahead Alert! Soak the bamboo skewers in water overnight to prevent the meat from sticking.

What to do:

Preparing the shrimp:
Combine the coconut and bread crumbs in a shallow baking dish larger than 8 inches, and mix well. Combine the flour and the Creole seasoning into another shallow baking dish of equal size, and mix well. Place the beaten eggs into a third baking dish of the same size.

Slide the shrimp onto 8-inch bamboo skewers. Dredge the shrimp, first in the flour mixture, then in the beaten eggs, and finally in the bread crumb-coconut mixture, shaking off any excess ingredients after each step. Lay the shrimp skewers on a greased baking sheet so that they do not touch each other.

Heat several inches of oil to 360°F in a deep pan or electric fryer. Fry the shrimp in batches until golden brown and cooked through, about 3 to 4 minutes per batch. Drain on paper towels.

Serve the shrimp with Creole Marmalade, in a small bowl, as a side.

Preparing the Creole Marmalade:
Combine the marmalade, horseradish, and mustard together in a bowl, and mix well.

Yield: 6 to 8 skewers

What you'll need:

For the shrimp:
2 cups shredded, sweet-ened coconut
2 cups Panko bread crumbs
2 tablespoons Creole seasoning
2 cups all-purpose flour
4 large eggs, beaten
24 large shrimp, peeled and deveined

Vegetable oil, for frying
8-inch bamboo skewers
Paper towels

For the Creole Marmalade:
1 cup orange marmalade
2 tablespoons prepared horseradish
2 tablespoon Creole or whole-grain mustard

Creole-Barbecued Oysters

What you'll need:

For the Creole Barbecue Sauce:
1 cup Frank's® RedHot® Original hot sauce
1/4 cup honey
1/4 pound butter, cut into small chunks

For the fried oysters:
6 oysters shucked
2 ounces Creole Barbecue Sauce (see recipe below)
Vegetable oil, for frying
1 cup flour, seasoned with 2 tablespoons Creole seasoning
Prepared bleu cheese dressing

What to do:

Preparing the Creole Barbecue Sauce
(To be prepared before shucking the oysters):
Heat hot sauce and honey together in a pot, and bring to a boil. Whisk in the butter until melted and remove from heat. Cover to keep the sauce warm.

Preparing the fried oysters:
Shuck and drain the oysters. Coat the oysters with the seasoned flour and shake off any excess. Heat up the oil on the stove or in an electric fryer, and deep-fry the oysters until golden brown, about 3 to 4 minutes.

Arrange the reserved oyster shells on a dinner plate. Place 2 ounces of the prepared barbecue sauce in a bowl and coat each fried oyster thoroughly with sauce. Plate the oysters, top with the bleu cheese dressing, and serve.

Yield: about 2 servings

Breeding habits of the Native Oyster involves a series of successive alternations of sex, each individual changing from male to female and back again several times during its lifetime. Some of those in the process of changing may be considered intersex, operating for a short time as both male and female.

Served hot on the half-shell from which they were shucked, these oysters cook up a lot like chicken wings, 'cept they don't have to be plucked.

Papricot Chicken

Spice up the chicken in your life with a dash of apricot. Who needs toast when you have chicken breast to spread it on? Add curry and jam and everyone will feel like chicken tonight.

What you'll need:

1/2 cup canned apricot nectar
3/4 cup amber ale
3 tablespoons apricot fruit spread
2 teaspoons paprika
1 teaspoon hot curry powder
4 skinless, boneless chicken breasts, thawed and slightly hammered
Salt, to taste
Freshly ground black pepper, to taste

What to do:

Preheat the oven to 325°F. Combine the apricot nectar, amber ale, fruit spread, paprika, and curry powder in a mixing bowl. Whisk well to blend.

Place the chicken breasts in a ceramic casserole dish and cover with the apricot blend. Bake for 35 to 45 minutes. Turn the breasts twice while cooking to avoid dry, withered-breast syndrome. Season the breasts with salt and pepper.

For a nice finish, warm up a small amount of the apricot fruit spread and spoon a dollop of it on top of the breasts for the last five minutes of cooking.

Yield: will serve 2 fat boys or 4 hungry cheerleaders

Cajun-Blackened Halibut

What you'll need:

- 1 teaspoon salt
- 1 teaspoon minced fresh thyme
- 1/2 teaspoon dry oregano
- 1/2 teaspoon cayenne pepper
- 1/2 teaspoon sweet paprika
- 1/2 teaspoon freshly ground black pepper
- 1/2 teaspoon crushed fennel seeds
- 4 6-ounce halibut fillets
- 2 tablespoons olive oil
- 4 teaspoons butter

What to do:

Preheat the oven to 400°F. Combine the salt, thyme, oregano, cayenne pepper, paprika, black pepper, and fennel seeds in a mixing bowl. Mix well. Place the fillets on a baking sheet and brush both sides with 1 tablespoon of the oil. Sprinkle each fillet with the seasoning mixture.

Place a large skillet on high heat until very hot. Add the remaining oil and swirl to coat the skillet completely. Place the fillets in the skillet, seasoned-side down and cook for about 1 minute, or until brown. Return the fillets to the baking sheet, browned-side up. Bake in the oven for about 8 minutes, or until opaque. Top each fillet with 1 tablespoon of butter and serve.

Yield: 4 servings

The Pacific halibut was called "haly-butte" in Middle English, meaning the flatfish to be eaten on holy days.

Like the old saying goes:

Blacken your fish and burn your

mouth, this dish will take you

deep down South.

Spareribs

Got some spare time?
Warm up your guests while
you're watching the game with
these rib-tickling rib-stickers.

Did you know that if you make your own muffins and some other baked goods, you may replace up to half the oil or fat with applesauce or other pureed fruit to reduce the fat calories?

What you'll need:

6 pounds spareribs
3 cups applesauce
6 cups brown sugar
1 1/2 cups freshly squeezed lemon juice
1 1/2 teaspoons salt
1 1/2 teaspoons freshly ground black pepper
1 1/2 teaspoons paprika
1 1/2 teaspoons garlic powder
1 1/2 teaspoons cinnamon

What to do:

Preheat the oven to 350°F. Combine the applesauce, brown sugar, lemon juice, salt, pepper, paprika, garlic powder, and cinnamon in a heavy saucepan, and stir. Cook over medium-high heat, and bring to a boil. Cook for about 2 minutes, stirring often to avoid sticking.

Place the ribs in a baking dish and brush them with the sauce. Bake for 2 hours, turning and basting occasionally.

Yield: 6 servings

GAMBLING

On February 3, 2006, the Las Vegas Strip rolled out the orange carpet to welcome Hooters® Casino Hotel (formerly The Hotel San Remo) to its prestigious list of must-see, go-to places. Hooters® decided to lay a bet on the table that our fans would consider this casino hotel a winner—and they do! Was it those world famous, beautiful Hooters® Girls? You will just have to go to find out for yourself!

Visitors and guests alike are invited to chow down and chill out with delicious food and drink offerings from nine fine-to-funky restaurants and bars, ranging from world famous wing joint, Hooters® Restaurant, to Porch Dogs' rocking poolside bar, Dan Marino's Fine Food & Spirits, and the sophisticated 13 Martini Bar. You will also not want to miss the locals' new favorite, Shorty Burgers, found only at Pete & Shorty's Book and Bar. For great sushi, it's The Bait Shoppe, and for old-fashioned comfort food, head over to The Dam Restaurant, a 24/7 retro-style diner named after that other attraction not far from Vegas.

In keeping with the now-famous Hooters'® casual beach theme, the location's pool area features sand, palm trees, a lagoon waterfall, colorful lounges and seating, and Nipper's Pool Bar. Check out the deliciously dangerous Nipper's Juice! And don't say we didn't warn you.

For overnight guests, 696 island-casual rooms and awesome Hooters®-style suites offer cool comfort away from the hustle and bustle of Vegas. We started with some of the most comfortable beds we could find and then topped them off with top quality sheets and blankets, along with plush, luxurious towels. After a good night's sleep, head over to S.A.S.S., our salon and spa. The latest and greatest exercise equipment meets the most talented group of hot stylists, nail experts, and massage therapists.

Visit Hooters® Casino Hotel today and you'll soon see why we say it is "The Cure for the Common Casino!"

Know the TERMS

Ready to play with the big boys?
Better brush up on the nicknames
of Texas Hold 'Em hands...

A-A	Rockets; Bullets; American Airlines	A-K	Big Slick	10-5	Five and Dime
K-K	Cowboys	A-Q	Big Chick; Walking Back to Houston	10-4	Convoy; Good Buddy
Q-Q	Ladies; Siegfried & Roy	A-J	Blackjack	10-2	Texas Dolly
J-J	Fishhooks; Hooks	A-10	Bookends	9-8	Oldsmobile
8-8	Snowmen; Doggie Balls	A-8	Dead Man's Hand	9-6	Big Lick; Dinner for Two
7-7	Sunset Strip	K-Q	Marriage	9-5	Dolly Parton
6-6	Route 66	K-J	Kojak	9-2	Montana Banana
5-5	Presto; Speed Limit	K-9	Fido; What a Dog	8-3	Most feared hand in Holdem
4-4	Sailboats	K-3	Commander Crab; King Crab	7-10	Split
3-3	Crabs	Q-7	Computer hand	7-6	Union Oil
2-2	Ducks	J-5	Motown; Jackson Five	7-2	Beer Hand
				5-7	Heinz

Cajun Shrimp Bake

Whoo-eeeee, them's good eats!

What you'll need:

1/4 cup butter
1 small red onion, chopped
1/2 cup chopped red bell pepper
1/2 cup chopped yellow bell pepper
1/2 cup chopped green bell pepper
4 garlic cloves, minced
1 tablespoon freshly squeezed lemon juice
1 1/2 teaspoons salt
2 pounds pink baby shrimp, thawed
1 (10 3/4-ounce) can cream of shrimp soup
1/2 cup dry white wine
1 tablespoon soy sauce
1/2 teaspoon cayenne pepper
3 cups cooked long-grain white rice
1/4 cup grated Parmesan cheese
Parsley, for garnish
Lemon slices, for garnish

What to do:

Preheat the oven to 350°F.

Melt the butter in a large skillet over medium-high heat. Add the onion, bell peppers, and garlic and sauté for about 1 minute. Stir in the lemon juice and salt, and sauté for another 5 minutes. Add the shrimp and cook for 3 minutes, or until pink. Stir in the soup, wine, soy sauce, cayenne pepper, and rice until mixed thoroughly.

Pour the mixture into a lightly greased 11 by 7-inch baking dish. Sprinkle the Parmesan evenly over the top. Bake for 15 to 20 minutes, or until the cheese is bubbly and slightly browned. Garnish with parsley and lemon slices.

Yield: 8 to 10 servings

Tip for the fancy boy:

Try garnishing with a dollop of sour cream and a few cooked baby shrimp, as shown.

Spicy Beef & Pepper Jack Quiche

Whoever said, "Real men don't eat quiche" obviously never tried this one. We say, "Are you man enough to eat it?"

What you'll need:

1 9-inch unbaked pie shell
3/4 cup shredded colby or Cheddar cheese
3/4 cup shredded pepper Jack cheese
1/8 cup chopped jalapeños
1/4 cup chopped green chiles
1 1/2 cups cooked and finely chopped roast beef or steak
1 cup heavy cream
4 eggs
1/8 teaspoon ground cumin
1/4 teaspoon salt
1/4 teaspoon black pepper
Paprika, for garnish

What to do:

Preheat the oven to 325°F. Thaw and prepare the pie shell according to the package directions. Remove the shell from its tin and place it in a 9-inch, deep-dish, glass pie plate. Press it firmly into place.

Combine the cheeses, chiles, and beef in a medium bowl and mix well. Spoon the mixture into the bottom of the pie crust. Reuse the bowl and whisk in the cream, eggs, cumin, salt, and black pepper. Pour over the beef, chili, and cheese mixture.

Place the quiche in the oven and bake for 55 to 60 minutes, or until it doesn't stick when poked with a knife. Cut into wedges, garnish with paprika, and serve.

Yield: 6 servings

Turkey & Cheese Quiche

Cook this up the day after Thanksgiving,
then watch the family gobble up the leftovers.

What you'll need:

- 1 cup whipping cream
- 4 eggs
- 1/4 teaspoon salt
- 1/4 teaspoon white pepper
- 2 tablespoons chopped onion
- 1 cup diced cooked turkey
- 1 9-inch unbaked pie shell
- 1 cup shredded Swiss cheese

What to do:

Preheat the oven to 375°F.

Beat the whipping cream, eggs, salt, pepper, and onion together in a small bowl.

Arrange the turkey pieces in the bottom of the pie shell. Sprinkle the Swiss cheese over the turkey. Pour the creamy egg mixture over the turkey and cheese. Bake the quiche for 35 to 40 minutes, or until it doesn't stick when poked with a knife. Cut it into wedges and serve.

Yield: 4 servings

Tip: Add your favorite veggies to this recipe and your guests will be super impressed.

107

Dungeness Crab Fried Rice

Next time you serve your guests fish, get more creative than adding
a bottle of white wine. Packed to the gills with succulent crab meat,
this dish makes for a whale of a side.

What you'll need:

1/4 cup salad oil
1 heaping tablespoon chopped garlic
2 teaspoons grated fresh ginger
1/4 chopped green onions, to be added at the beginning
1/2 teaspoon red pepper flakes
1 cup minced yellow onions
1 cup finely chopped carrots
1 cup diced ham
4 cups cooked white rice
1/2 cup oyster sauce
1/4 cup soy sauce
2 tablespoons sesame oil
2 tablespoons sugar
2 pounds Dungeness crab
1 3-egg omelet, cooled and diced
3/4 cup chopped green onions, to be added at the very end

What to do:

Heat the salad oil in a wok or large frying pan over high heat. Add the garlic, ginger, 1/4 cup of the green onions, and red pepper flakes; and cook, stirring continuously to prevent the ingredients from browning. Add the onions, carrots, and ham and stir-fry until done.

Add the stir-fried mixture to the cooked rice in a large mixing bowl and mix thoroughly. Add the oyster sauce, soy sauce, sesame oil, and sugar and stir to mix well. Pour into a large skillet and cook for 1 to 2 minutes. Gently fold in the crab meat and the cooked omelet and cook until heated through. Add in the remaining green onions and serve.

Yield: 4 servings

Lynne Austin's Lucky 7-Layer Salad

Lynne Austin, the Original Hooters® Girl, says, "This salad is perfect for everything from a Super Bowl party to a PTA meeting."

 Plan Ahead Alert! You will need to refrigerate the salad for 24 hours before serving.

What to do:

Preparing the dressing:
In a small bowl, blend together the ranch dressing, sugar, and mayonnaise. Set aside.

Assembling the salad:
In a large glass salad bowl, lay the romaine lettuce down in the bottom. Then layer on the cheese, bacon, peas, chopped eggs, and green onions. Pour the dressing on top.

Garnish with green onions, if desired. Cover and refrigerate for 24 hours before serving.

Variations to make it an 8, 9, or 10 layer salad: Try adding diced black olives, chopped tomatoes, or canned fried Chinese noodles.

Yield: 8 to10 servings

What you'll need:

For the dressing:
1/2 cup prepared Ranch Dressing
2 tablespoons granulated sugar
1/2 cup mayonnaise

For the salad:
1 store-bought bag chopped romaine lettuce
1 8-ounce package shredded cheddar cheese
8 slices bacon, crisp-cooked and chopped
1 10-ounce package frozen green peas
4 hard-boiled eggs, chopped
4 to 5 green onions, trimmed and sliced

Crawfish Boil

Down in Louisiana, a crawfish boil is a social gathering that brings together friends and family during the bountiful crawfish harvest of the Louisiana deltas. The size of the boil can range from 20 pounds of live crawfish to hundreds of pounds for large events. The following recipe is for approximately 35 to 40 pounds of live crawfish which we cook in a 60 to 80-quart pot. The "boil" includes many other optional ingredients that make a great "one-pot" meal, including onions, garlic, corn on the cob, smoked sausage, and new potatoes that absorb the great flavor of the spices.

Since everyone may not have a 60 to 80-quart pot available, use the largest pot you have and adjust the level of the ingredients to fit your pot.

Fill the pot approximately 2/3 full of water and bring to a boil. While the water is heating, clean the live crawfish by soaking them in fresh water for 5 to 10 minutes. Drain the water from the crawfish and repeat this process 3 or 4 times to thoroughly clean/rinse them. Drain the crawfish and set aside. Pick out any dead crawfish and discard.

When the water comes to a rolling boil, add the following:

> 4 pounds Cajun's Choice® Shrimp, Crab & Crawfish Boil spice
> 4 lemons, cut in half
> 4 whole garlic bulbs
> 2 to 3 pounds small (golf-ball sized) onions
> 2 to 3 pounds small red potatoes (golf-ball sized preferred)

Cook for another 10 minutes, and add live crawfish and bring back to a boil.

Cook for 2 to 3 minutes. Turn off the burner or remove from heat, and add 15 short ears of corn on the cob and push them down into the water.

Let the whole shebang steep in the seasoned water for 5 to 10 minutes. NOTE: The longer it steeps, the spicier the flavor.

Carefully drain the hot water out. Pour the drained contents onto a table covered with newspaper. Gather around the table and enjoy!

For boiled shrimp, follow the same instructions as above, but only cook the shrimp 1 to 2 minutes and let steep for 3 to 5 minutes being careful not to overcook them. Overcooked shrimp are much harder to peel.

For boiled Blue crabs, cook for 5 minutes and steep 10 minutes. For boiled Dungeness crabs, cook for 12 minutes and steep for 10 minutes.

Dirt Pie

When a hog has an itch on his back, he scratches it by rolling in the dirt. When you have an itch in your sweet tooth, we recommend you scratch it by letting it roll around in this deliciously dirty Dirt Pie.

What you'll need:

1 package cream-filled chocolate sandwich cookies
1/2 stick butter, softened
1 cup sugar
8 ounces cream cheese
2 boxes instant vanilla pudding
3 1/2 cups milk
12 ounces frozen whipped topping

What to do:

Chop the cookies in a food processor until they look like dirt. Mix the butter, cream cheese, and sugar by hand in a mixing bowl until smooth. Blend the pudding, milk, and frozen whipped topping together separately. Combine the two mixtures, stirring until the lumps are gone. Layer the cookie dirt and the creamy mixture in a 9 by 13-inch glass baking pan, alternating layers until all the ingredients are in the pan. Chill and serve.

Yield: 8 to 10 servings

Toffee Apple Dip

Next time the kids are nagging for a snack, try putting these sticky treats in their busy mouths.

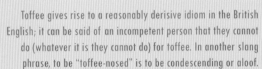

Toffee gives rise to a reasonably derisive idiom in the British English; it can be said of an incompetent person that they cannot do (whatever it is they cannot do) for toffee. In another slang phrase, to be "toffee-nosed" is to be condescending or aloof.

What you'll need:

1 8-ounce package cream cheese
1/2 cup brown sugar
1/3 cup white sugar
1 teaspoon vanilla
1 bag toffee candy bits
Apple slices (Granny Smiths recommended)

What to do:

Whisk or blend together the cream cheese, brown sugar, white sugar, vanilla, and candy bits in a medium-sized bowl until smooth. Chill. Serve with fresh apple slices.

Yield: 1 1/2 cups dip

Green Bay Packed Peanut Butter Balls

Chatty football fans interrupting the game? Stick their tongues to the roofs of their mouths with these sweet, sweet clusters.

In 1890, an enterprising physician, Dr. John Kellogg, of the corn-flake empire, created peanut butter as a healthy protein substitute that was easy to digest for patients with no teeth. With or without teeth, peanut butter is a high-protein treat.

What you'll need:

1 cup crunchy peanut butter
1 cup chocolate chips
1/2 cup instant nonfat dry milk
3 tablespoons water
Shredded coconut (or chopped peanuts)

What to do:

Mix the peanut butter, chocolate chips, dry milk, and water thoroughly in a bowl. Form the mixture into golf-ball sized balls. Roll each ball in the shredded coconut or chopped peanuts and serve.

Yield: 12 golf-ball sized peanut-butter balls

Rockin' Cocktails

Medium, Hot, or 911 Hooters® Mary

The perfect rescue from those 3-alarm hangovers.

What you'll need:
- 1 1/4 ounces Smirnoff® Bloody Mary Mix
- 4 ounces tomato juice
- 3 dashes Worcestershire sauce
- 3/4 teaspoon shrimp boil
- 1, 3, or 5 dashes Hooters® Hot Sauce
- 4 shakes black pepper
- 1 celery stick
- 1 lime wedge

Hooters® Cocktail Tip: For extra flavor, we recommend coating the rim of the glass with a little shrimp boil.

What to do:
Fill a cocktail glass with ice. Pour the Bloody Mary mix, tomato juice, Worcestershire sauce, shrimp boil, and the appropriate amount of hot sauce in a mixing tin. Add ice from the glass, cap with a mixing tin and shake for approximately 3 seconds. Pour the mix into the glass. Dip in a celery stick and place a lime wedge on the rim of the glass. Throw in a straw and serve it up.

Blonde Bombshell Martini

Remember, blondes have more fun, and you will too with this beauty by your side.

What you'll need:
- 1/2 ounce Smirnoff® Vodka
- 1/2 ounce Bailey's® Irish Cream
- 1/2 ounce Kahlúa®
- 1/2 ounce Grand Marnier®
- 1 ounce half & half
- 1 orange twist

What to do:
Chill a cocktail glass prior to serving. Fill a mixing glass 2/3 full with cubed ice. Pour the Smirnoff® Vodka, Bailey's®, Kahlúa®, Grand Marnier®, and half & half into the mixing glass. Cap with a mixing tin and shake for 4 seconds. Strain the liquid into the chilled cocktail glass, garnish with the orange twist, and serve.

Key Lime Pie Martini

This one will have you seeing pies in the sky.

What you'll need:
- 1 1/4 ounces Captain Morgan's® Spiced Rum
- 1 1/2 ounces Island Oasis® Margarita Mix
- 1 1/2 ounces half & half
- 2 teaspoons sugar
- 1 lime wedge

What to do:
Chill a cocktail glass prior to serving. Fill a mixing glass 2/3 full with cubed ice. Pour the spiced rum, margarita mix, half & half, and sugar into a mixing glass. Cap with a mixing tin and shake for 4 seconds. Strain the liquid into the chilled cocktail glass, garnish with the lime wedge, and serve.

Christmas Light Lemonade

Ho, ho, ho! This one's just right after a day in the snow!

What you'll need:
- 1 1/4 ounces Absolut® Citron
- 3/4 ounce Sour Apple Schnapps
- 1 maraschino cherry
- 1 lime wedge, unsqueezed
- 1 lemon wedge, unsqueezed
- 1 orange wedge, unsqueezed
- 3 ounces lemonade

What to do:
Fill a cocktail glass with ice. Pour the Absolut® Citron, Sour Apple Schnapps, cherry, citrus wedges, and lemonade into a mixing tin. Add ice from the glass, cap with a mixing tin and shake for approximately 3 seconds. Pour the mix into the cocktail glass and serve.

Iced Tea

This might surprise some fast-food addicts, but just in case you didn't know, here's a little secret about iced tea: you can make it yourself. Here's how:

What you'll need:

Water
6 teabags (black tea works best)
1 cup sugar
1/2 of a lemon

What to do:

Bring 1 1/2 quarts of water to a boil in a saucepan. Remove the pan from the heat and add the teabags, making sure they are submerged, and steep for 8 to 10 minutes. Add the sugar and 1 cup of cold water in a large pitcher. Remove the teabags and pour the tea into the pitcher. Squeeze in the lemon and stir well. Serve chilled or on ice.

Yield: 1 pitcher

Hooterberry Lemonade

Never heard of Hooterberries?
Neither have we, but they sound good, don't they?

What you'll need:

1 1/2 cups freshly squeezed lemon juice
6 cups cold water
10 ounces puréed fresh or frozen strawberries
Sugar, to taste
Ice
6 lemon slices, for garnish

What to do:

Combine the lemon juice, water, and 3/4 of the strawberry purèe in a large pitcher. Add sugar to taste. Add the remaining strawberry purèe until the strawberry and lemon flavors are balanced.

Serve over ice and garnish the glasses with lemon slices.

Yield: 6 servings

Bleu Hawaiian Salad

What you'll need:

4 cups romaine lettuce
1/2 cup strawberries
1/2 cup seedless grapes
1/2 cup bite-sized orange pieces
1/2 cup bite-sized honeydew pieces
1/2 cup bite-sized cantaloupe pieces
1/2 cup chopped pineapple
1/4 cup Naturally Fresh® Bleu Cheese Dressing
1/4 cup Naturally Fresh® Fat-Free Raspberry Vinaigrette

What to do:

Combine the lettuce, strawberries, grapes, orange, honeydew, cantaloupe, and pineapple in a large salad bowl. Mix the Naturally Fresh® Bleu Cheese Dressing with the Naturally Fresh® Fat-Free Raspberry Vinaigrette and pour on top of the salad. Toss well and serve chilled.

Yield: 4 servings

Caribbean Chicken Salad

What you'll need:

3 quarts mixed salad greens
2 cups seedless grapes
2 cups shredded carrots
1 small can Mandarin oranges, drained
2 cups white raisins
1/4 cup Naturally Fresh® Fat-Free Raspberry Vinaigrette
2 whole boneless, skinless chicken breasts
2 tablespoons lemon juice
1 cup water
2 cups pineapple chunks, drained

What to do:

Combine the mixed greens, grapes, carrots, oranges (reserve a few for garnish), and white raisins with 1/4 cup of Naturally Fresh® Fat-Free Raspberry Vinaigrette. Marinate the chicken in lemon juice and water, then sauté in a medium frying pan until done. Add the pineapple chunks to sauté for one minute. Transfer the chicken and pineapple to the dressed salad. Garnish with Mandarin oranges and serve.

Yield: 8 servings

HOOTERS®

CULINARY ACADEMY

Having successfully completed the prescribed course of instruction by firing up at least one grill and preparing at least one recipe from Recipes to Impress, this diploma is awarded to:

_____

in recognition of the completion of Man Cooking, Hooters® Style.

Hootie

Chef Hootie, Dean of Man Food

If you would like information about purchasing Hooters® products (such as the Hooters® MasterCard®, *Hooters® Magazine*, the Hooters® Swimsuit Calendar, apparel and gifts) go to:

www.Hooters.com

BUSINESS REPLY MAIL

FIRST-CLASS MAIL   PERMIT NO 1479   ANAHEIM CA

POSTAGE WILL BE PAID BY ADDRESSEE

**HOOTERS MAGAZINE
PO BOX 18479
ANAHEIM CA 92817-9933**

**NO POSTAGE
NECESSARY
IF MAILED
IN THE
UNITED STATES**

BUSINESS REPLY MAIL
FIRST-CLASS MAIL   PERMIT NO 1479   ANAHEIM CA

POSTAGE WILL BE PAID BY ADDRESSEE

**HOOTERS MAGAZINE
PO BOX 18479
ANAHEIM CA 92817-9933**